From the Playing Fields
to the Feds

JAMES HARRIS

Copyright © 2023 James Harris
All rights reserved
First Edition

PAGE PUBLISHING
Conneaut Lake, PA

First originally published by Page Publishing 2023

ISBN 979-8-88960-358-0 (pbk)
ISBN 979-8-88960-367-2 (digital)

Printed in the United States of America

Introduction

I'm the last man going to my cell tonight for lockdown. I'm going home in the morning and can't sleep a wink. I guess it's anxiety. I want to see my family and friends who've been with me throughout this prison term. I've done twenty-seven months of my life in the Feds.

"Lockdown, Harris… Good luck out there," said a CO, whom I don't even know by name, better yet by face.

I get a lot of that. I guess because I played in the NFL, I'm not treated as a human being. You are looked at as a tool or machine that is an asset to an organization, and when you're no longer durable and reliable to the team's standard, you're considered a liability and tossed to the side because you are no longer needed. Of course, there are exceptions for some players who are showed loyalty by their organization. That's why you must invest your money and have a nest egg, but I guess you could say that I had the right intentions but the wrong method. Since I can't sleep, I'm going to tell you how I went from playing the field to the Feds.

Chapter 1

Where it All Began

So, God created man in his own image; in the image of God, he created him.

—Genesis 1:27

I was born in East St. Louis on May 13, 1967. My mother, Katricia Harris, is a schoolteacher and my father, Roger Johnson, is a musician and hustler. My parents were high school sweethearts. Everybody in the neighborhood knew they would stay together forever. I was the firstborn out of the two sons they had. My brother, Eric Harris, is three years younger than me.

I grew up on State Street and was always around my grandmother. She was the backbone of the family. I had only two uncles. Uncle Peter was on my mother's side of the family, and Uncle James was on my father's side. I was named after Uncle James, and he became my favorite uncle. Instead of James, everybody called him Junebug, including me. Well, with the uncle in front.

In the seventies, my uncle Junebug was like a father to me because my father was in jail. He was the first man I looked up to and the coolest man I've ever known. He would come over my Grandmother Delores' house and always have something for me. He bought me my first pair of cleats to play Little League football.

My friends—Terry a.k.a. T. I., Douglass, a. m. Fats—were always with me, so when my uncle Junebug gave me money, I would give them some of it. They both didn't play sports, but that didn't stop us from hanging out 24-7. We had all the little girls liking us in school.

When I was in middle school, I was selling cocaine on the streets after school.

My uncle Junebug was the supplier, and I was the provider for the Southside, along with T. I. and Fathead. I liked the feeling of being able to provide for my family and friends. My mother used to always tell me that my weakness was I didn't know how to say no to the people I love or like.

One of my fondest memories as a child was when the Cowboys were playing the Broncos in the 1977 Super Bowl, and Butch Johnson made a one-handed catch for a touchdown. My mother was looking at the game with me in the living from on our floor model television set. I was stretched out on my stomach on the shag carpet while my mother was on the couch.

I raised up my upper torso with my elbows and said, "Ma, that's what I'm goin' ta' do the rest of my life and get paid. I'ma take care of ya' an' my friends."

"I believe anything you say" is what she said to me.

At middle school, I excelled in sports and played football, basketball, and baseball. I was outstanding in baseball as a center fielder, but I didn't like the sport. I was able to play sports, hustle, and still get good grades in school.

My drug clientele were the clean and respected people of the neighborhood. I would sell to most of my customers on the weekend. T. I. and Fats would help me out. They would even sell for me when I was at a game or practice. We called ourselves the three musketeers.

We were ballers at the age of thirteen. I had hundred grand to show for it in cash that I kept in sneaker boxes in my room closet. I stayed humble by attending church every Sunday and giving to charity. I read the Bible and said my prayers every night before going to bed. I always kept my faith in God even while I was doing wrong at a young age.

FROM THE PLAYING FIELDS TO THE FEDS

When I got into high school, I was popular even as a freshman. It was 1982 and I was rolling in a green Pontiac Lemans. My friends used to clown me about the ride but were the first to jump in it. My uncle Junebug had been sent to jail my freshman year for drugs, but my pops got me the car for my fifteenth birthday.

East St. Louis, a.k.a. East Boogie, was picking up a name for itself in the eighties for being high in crime. It was rated as the number one murder rate per capita in the world at the time. The population was only estimated around forty thousand people. Where there is a lot of self-hatred, you can find a lot of violence. Growing up in East Boogie made me aware of my surroundings. It was also known for having clubs that stayed open till the break of dawn. Gangsta Disciples and Vicelords were the gangs in the hood.

I attended Eastside High School which was down the block from my house. I stopped playing baseball and just stuck with basketball and football my freshman year. At the time, I was already six feet four. My coach, Bob Shannon, had heard I was playing basketball.

He saw me going to class one day in November and stopped me in the hallway and said, "Hey, Harris. Come by my office after your last-period class."

"I'll be there, Coach Shannon," I said.

After my English was over, I went to lock up my books in my locker when Michelle came up from behind me and said, "James, have you seen Rollo?"

Now Michelle had to know where Rollo was, but I went along with her game and said, "I can't say that I have."

"Well, he's s'ppose to drive me home. Can you drive?"

I looked at Michelle up and down. She had on some Jordache jeans that were hugging her legs. She had the prettiest brown eyes to go with her sandy-blond hair, which she wore hanging down to her shoulders.

"I can't. I got to go see what my coach wants."

"All right then. If you see…never mind," Michelle said, walking away with them Jordache jeans painted on her behind.

"Damn!" I said to myself, watching her walk away and disappearing into a sea of students in the corridor.

I made it over to the gym where Mr. Shannon's office was and knocked on the door. "Come in" was all I heard.

I went inside, and he stood up and said, "Sit down, Harris." Mr. Shannon wanted me to sit, so he could look down at me because he felt intimidated by my height. He walked around the desk and stood in front of me and said, "I don't need you playing no basketball while you're a quarterback on my team."

"But, Mr. Shannon—"

"But nothing. If you get hurt, there is no backup that can replace you."

"I'm not going to get hurt playing basketball."

"I know you're not because you're not playing."

"What if I decide to play basketball and not football?"

"Listen, Harris. You have the potential to go as far as you wanna go. I'm trying to help bring the best out of you."

I knew right then Coach Shannon and I were not going to get along. He wasn't going to be telling me what I shouldn't and should be doing.

My sophomore year was the same way. We argued all season. I decided to leave Eastside and transfer to Lincoln High School for my junior year. Coach Reynolds was much more understanding. I was the quarterback and played the center position in basketball with one of the best players out of East St. Louis named Laphonso Ellis. Our school had a good season in both sports. The only thing about the school I didn't like was that it was stricter. I had to stop bringing weed to school.

In May, I had a birthday party over at my grandma Delores' house and got so drunk that Michelle and I went upstairs and had sex in the bedroom I slept in.

It was the second week of summer, and the Fourth of July was about to come up when Michelle told me she was pregnant. She'd already had a son by Rollo. I knew I had made a mistake but was willing to take responsibility. Michelle knew she had a better man in me than in Rollo too.

On January 25, 1986, we had a boy and named him Kyle Harris. Later on in the same year, Laphonso Ellis and I took Lincoln High

School all the way to the state championships and won. Afterward, Michelle and I were inseparable. We were having sex like we were making porno movies. In the car, on top of the car in the movie theater, and once she even sat on my lap wearing a dress with no panties on right in front of my grandma's house. It was pure lust, but I thought it was love.

I got a scholarship to go to Temple University and threw a big party at my mother's house. Fats, T. I., and I got drunk and then when everybody left, we went and sat outside. It was about one in the morning. We were all dressed alike, wearing shorts and Top Ten Adidas.

"So ya' fit'na leave us, huh?" T. I. said.

"Yeah, man, but ya' know we're tight. I'm goin' to call for y'all as soon as I get there and let y'all kno' whassup," I said.

"I know you're not fit'na fogit us," Fats said.

"Nev'va that. You my nephews," I said, meaning every word of it.

Chapter 2

The City of Brotherly Love

Do not commit to anyone.

—Robert Greene

I arrived in Philadelphia by plane with only one big duffel bag. I immediately caught the train and got off at Girard and Broad and caught a cab to Temple University. Bear in mind that this is my first time away from home by myself. I was excited but nervous. When I got out of the cab, I was right in front of my dorm.

I made it up to my room on my own and started to unpack but then decided to go back downstairs and meet a few people I'd passed on my way up to the room. It was August and the weather was still hot. I was wearing some Polo jeans and a short-sleeved shirt along with moccasins. When I got back downstairs, there were the same dudes there talking loudly about football. I knew they had to be on the team.

"Whassup, man. You just came here, right?"

"Yeah, man," I said.

"Where you come from?"

"East St. Louis."

"Yeah. I'm Gumby from Memphis. And that's Floyd and Lonnie," he said, pointing to two other guys that were seated on a sofa.

I went and gave them both a quick handshake and told them my name.

"You play on the team?" Gumby asked.

"Yeah. I'm the new quarterback."

"Uh-oh. Pretty Tony got some competition," Lonnie said.

"Yo, Harris, do the coach know you're here?" asked Floyd.

"Nah. I just got here," I said.

"I'll take you over to the office," Gumby said.

We walked over to another building that was about a couple of blocks away. Temple University was a community within Philly. It had more students enrolled in the school than some town's population. And with Penn State Drexel, LaSalle, and Villanova in the vicinity, it made Philly larger than it seemed.

Gumby took me inside Macganabo Hall and past a desk in a corridor where there was an office. He knocked on the door, and I heard a female voice say, "Come in."

"Hey, Nadia. I just brought over someone who needs to see Coach Aarons."

"Okay, let me page him," she said. "And what's your name?"

"Harris...James Harris," I said as if I was James Bond to the prettiest Black lady I've ever laid eyes on.

"I'm Nadia. It's nice to meet you. My...you're very tall. You play basketball?"

"No," I said with a smile as the phone rang.

She picked it up and handled her business and turned her attention back to me. "He'll be over here in a little while. Have a seat," she said, getting up and walking over to a fax machine.

I sat down and couldn't help but look at her legs in that skirt. They were sculpted like a professional dancer.

"Where are you from?" she asked.

"I'm from East St. Louis."

"Ooh... I heard about there. It's between St. Louis Missouri and Illinois."

"It's in Illinois. St. Louis is right across the bridge."

"Oh, all right. Well, I'm from Philly. How do you like it so far?"

"I like what I see so far," I said, trying to flirt.

I could see Nadia was a little older than me. I was sizing her up and about to spit my game when Coach Aarons came in the door.

"I see you found your way around already," he said.

"Not really," I said, smiling. "One of the players brought me over here."

"So you do play football," Nadia said.

"Yeah. That's our new quarterback. Though I heard you can play basketball," Coach Aarons said.

"I bet it isn't too much he can't do," Nadia said.

I just stood there smiling and trying not to blush. This fine Black woman was throwing game back at me real smooth.

"I'm glad to see you made it here. I'll give you some time to go around the campus and will see you later. Maybe Nadia could show you around," he said.

"I could find some time to do that," she said.

"Well, let me know when you're ready," I said.

"Hold up," she said, looking at the calendar in the office. "I have some free time tomorrow."

"All right. I'll come over here and meet you at…"

"Make it eleven."

"No problem. Talk to you later, coach," I said, exiting the office.

The following day, I kept looking at my watch as I ran out of things to do in the morning. I was anxious to see Nadia again. When ten thirty came, I made my way over to Macganabo Hall. Nadia was on the phone when I entered the office. She looked up and smiled.

After a few minutes, she hung up the phone and said, "I see you're punctual. That's a good sign."

"Good sign of what?"

"That you are going to be a good date."

"This is a date?" I said inquisitively.

"If you want it to be. Let me grab my bag and we can go," she said.

We took the train all over Philly. We stopped by the famous Philly Cheesesteak House and ate. I learned the best way to learn a new city is by walking or using its transit system. Nadia explained every stop on the train to me. I enjoyed her accent and company. She was of Ethiopian descent. She had the prettiest skin tone I've seen with the smile to match. She was wifey material.

When we got back to the university, it was almost four o'clock. Time had gone by so fast with her that I didn't pay it too much attention.

"Where do you live at?" I said while we were walking back to the building.

"I stay on the south side. Chelton Avenue."

"By yourself?" I asked her and hoping I wasn't being too presumptuous.

"No. With my two-year-old son," she said.

We got back in the office, and I watched her put her MCM bag down before I said, "Thanks for the tour."

"No problem. I wanted to do that," she said, sitting down and smiling. Then she started laughing.

"What's so funny?"

"Your accent, you sound country."

"I'm not from round here," I said, laying it on thick.

She laughed some more and said, "I like it."

"I'll see ya' later."

"I hope so," she said, smiling at me as I left.

The following weekend, we had football practice. There was an out-of-conference game coming up, and I knew I wouldn't see no playing time unless the first stringer got hurt or if it was a blowout. Pretty Tony was the man. It was going to be hard to take his spot.

We played East Carolina. This was supposed to be a sure win. The game started out a little rough and tight to score in the first half. We were only up two field goals at the half. When we came out of the locker room at halftime, we played conservative by running the ball and letting our defense take control.

I was put in the game in the fourth quarter and threw for one completion out of four attempts. It was a ten-yard pass for a first down to our best receiver, Leslie Shepard. We won the game easily.

The following week, I went to school and everybody in my classes were speaking to me. One of my favorite classes was psychology because I sat next to this fine chocolate-complexion girl named

Nicole. Everybody called her Nikki. We would always say hi to each other and that's it…but not this week.

I entered the class just before it started and saw her about to sit down. She was wearing a nice Benetton outfit with some Patton leather shoes on. Her calves were looking right. Her hair had some extensions in them, and they looked good too.

"Hello, Nikki," I said as I approached her.

"How you are doing, James? I heard y'all won. Wish I could have seen it."

"Yeah. It was an easy game."

"I'll be at the homecoming game."

"That's in two weeks against Virginia Tech," I said, sitting down.

"I know. You going to the party?"

"I'll be thurr," I said as the professor came in the class.

*****

That night, I was sitting in the dorm and decided to call home. I hadn't talked to my friends since I'd gotten down here, so I went in the hallway and got on the phone and called my house collect. I heard my mother pick up the phone and accept.

"Hello, James. You aiight?"

"Yeah. I just called to say hello. Is Li'l E thurr?"

"Yeah. He just came in a li'l while ago. Hold on," she said as I heard her yelling his name to pick up the phone.

I heard the other end pick up, and I said, "Whassup, bro."

"Let me leave you two," my mother said, hanging up the phone.

"Whassup, big bro. Everybody said you ain't been calling."

"I kno'. That's why I wanted to holla at ya'. Call Fats and hook us up on the three-way."

"Aiight. Hold up," he said, clicking over.

I waited a few minutes and heard the phone click back over.

"Bro?"

"I'm here," I said, hearing the phone ringing.

"Hello."

"Wassup wit'chu," I said, knowing it was Fats on the other end.

"Wassup, kinfolk! I thought ya' forgot 'bout ya' boy."
"Nah. I can't do that thurr. I had to get settled."
"So how ya' like it down thurr?"
"It reminds me of East Boogie…just bigga."
"Yeah, that's cool. Everybody was wonderin' whassup wit'chu, man."
"I'm hangin' in thurr."
"What's dat noise I hear?"
"I'm in the hallway of my dorm usin' tha phone. Dem thurr is some girls ya' hearing."
"Damn! They fine?"
"Hell yeah."
"Hook ya' boy up then."
"Out of sight, out of mind. You ain't here. Tell T. I. I said whassup. I'm done on the three-way and don't want to burn up my mom's line."
"Aiight then. I'm fit'na go back out and check him anyhow."
"Aiight then later," I said as Fats hung up.
"Eric. You thurr?"
"Yeah."
"Thanks, bro. You aiight?"
"Yeah."
"Well, I'll talk ta' ya' later," I said before I hung up the phone.

When I get back to my room, my roommate was there. His name was Jeffery Hall. He was a short light-skinned square from Delaware.

"What's goin' on, Harris. I haven't see you all day."
"Yeah. I've been busy and I'm tired as hell," I said.
"Me too but I gotta get an hour in on this book for English class before I go to sleep."
"I hear ya'. I'm a goner," I said, going over to my bed and leaving him by the little table and lamp to read.

*****

The week before homecoming game, I was in psychology class.

When it ended, Nikki said, "Are you ready for this test next week?"

"Not really. But I'll be by next week."

"You can come by my room, and we can study. I'll be in there all this week. You know where I stay, right?"

"Yeah, I know," I said, picking up my books.

"I'll talk to you later, James."

"Aiight," I said, watching her ass move in her Guess jeans.

It was almost eleven when I made it over to the cafeteria. I saw my man, Gumby, in his usual spot and went over to him.

"Whassup, Gumby," I said over the loud talking.

"Hey! What up, Harris. I want you to meet my man here named Salaam."

"What up," Salaam said.

"What up," I said, extending my hand.

We embraced each other, and for some reason, I knew we were going to click. He worked in the cafeteria and was selling food for a discount. I'd seen him walking around the dorm shooting dice with the other guys too. A natural-born hustler. Salaam didn't stay in the dorms because he was from Philly. While we were talking, he asked me if wanted to hang out with him this weekend.

"Yeah. Show me some real clubs," I said.

"Don't worry. I will. I am Philly," he said with confidence.

Friday night came and Salaam took me out to a strip club called Knights on Broadway. He knew the manager and damn near all the strippers. I could tell he came here all the time because at the bar, they gave him Hennessey without him even asking.

A dark slim lanky dude with a high-top fade came over by us with a blunt in his hand and said, "Yo, Salaam. Ya' tryna go?"

"Yeah. Ayo, Bakim, this is my man from school named James. He's on the football team."

"What up," Bakim said, giving me a quick handshake (pound) with a ring on every finger.

I nodded and said, "Whassup."

"Let's go up in VIP," Salaam said, leading the way.

Salaam stopped by a Mexican man who was standing by the VIP entrance and started talking. Then he pointed toward me and Bakim.

While we went up and sat down in a corner of the room, Salaam came up right behind us with three scantily dressed girls. Salaam introduced then to me as Desire, Bootiful, and Mahogany as they handed some Hennessey on the rocks to us. I was liking Mahogany the best out of all of them. She had a nice dark-skinned complexion with an authentic glow and bedroom eyes. Desire and Bootiful were both light-skinned and short with big asses.

As I was just about to finish my Hennessey, Salaam said, "Yo, Harris, you want another drink?"

"Yeah."

"Why don y'all go get us some more drinks," Salaam said.

"We're not bartenders," Desire said.

"Yeah, but we are paying you to do it," Bakim said, pulling out a knot of money.

The girls scampered away to get the drinks, except Mahogany, who rolled her eyes and then walked away.

"Who do you like the best?" Salaam asked.

"Mahogany," I said.

"Aiight. That's who you got," Salaam said as he lit a blunt up. "You smoke?"

"Nah. Not no more," I said, trying to sound like I used to.

"You wanna try it?"

"Nah, but I wouldn't mind buying some to sell on the campus."

I got Bakim and Salaam's attention when I said this. Salaam immediately started coughing off the Philly blunt he'd rolled. This was my first time seeing weed rolled up like this.

Salaam passed the blunt to Bakim and said, "How much you wanna buy?"

"Forty pounds if I can."

This answer got the same response from Bakim who started coughing. Either that or that it was some good weed. I assumed it wasn't the latter...

"What ya' doin' tomorrow?" Salaam asked.

"Nothing," I said, which was a lie. I had to study and practice, but I could study with Nikki on Sunday.

"I'm goin' to take you to my connection. He's the Mexican you just seen. He stays over in Germantown. You don't kno' yo' way around that good, do you?"

"Nah."

"Don't worry, I'll shu' ya' the ropes," Salaam said as the girls were on their way back with drinks.

The rest of the night went smoothly. I got a lap dance from Mahogany and got her seven digits.

*****

It was 10:00 a.m. on Sunday when my roommate woke me up.

"Harris. Somebody's on the phone for you in the hall."

I rolled over and said, "Who is it?"

"She didn't say."

"Tell Nikki I'll be over there round five," I said, trying to go back to sleep.

"Aiight," Jeff said.

I knew it had to be Nikki. She probably thought I've been avoiding her.

*****

I bought fifty pounds of weed from the Mexican and another fifty pounds he gave me on consignment. Salaam was smiling and glad that he played a part by introducing us. After getting a hundred pounds, I came back to the dorm and bagged up some dimes and sold a few fifty pieces in the dorm. Then I went out clubbing with Salaam and didn't get back in until five in the morning.

That following day, I woke up after two o'clock. I took a shower, got dressed, and went to Kentucky Fried Chicken (KFC) before going over to Nikki's room. She was wearing some tight jeans and a Temple University T-shirt. I could see her nipples through the shirt.

"I bought us something to eat."

"You must've been reading my mind," Nikki said.

We ate and conversed. We got to know each other a little better. Nikki was majoring as a medical student.

After we finished eating, Nikki threw the boxes away and sat down next to me. She was staring at me while I was looking over her psychology notes.

"Whassup? Why are you staring at me like that?"

"I can't believe that your major is really elementary education."

"Yeah. My mother is a teacher, and that inspired me to wanting to help children too."

Right then I knew I had her mind if not her heart. While I studied for the psychology test, Nikki was getting touchy feely with me. By nightfall, her nipples were protruding through her T-shirt, and I had a semi-hard erection in my sweatpants that I wasn't trying to hide.

We started kissing, and it seemed like we were kissing for almost an hour. I had her jeans halfway down and my fingers inside her. She started moaning, thrusting her hips, and licking her lips as I pushed my fingers deeper into her.

"Ooh…James! Stop before you start something you can't finish. My roommate is going to be here soon," she said, breathing hard.

I could tell she was ready to go because she was still thrusting her pelvis on my hand. I could feel her insides getting wetter. I didn't stop until I felt her cum.

"Let me stop before we get caught by your roommate," I said, pulling my fingers out of her.

Nikki looked at me and was blushing. She got up and went to the bathroom, and I waited for her to come back out, so I could wash my hands. I knew she would think we were an item now. I could see it in her eyes as she came out of the bathroom. After I washed my hands, I came out of the bathroom, gave her a kiss, and left.

The weekend came quickly. Our homecoming game was a success. We played Virginia Tech and beat them. I got in the game in the fourth quarter. My highlight was when I ran for fifteen yards off a broken pass play. We were in the locker room and all everyone was talking about was the homecoming party.

Gumby and I went to the party together. We were dressed casually in jeans and loafers. I had on an Andrew Marc leather jacket and a Louis Vuitton pouch around my neck filled with dime bags of weed. I'd sold about twenty-five pounds of weed, and this was my first week on the campus.

When we got to Temple Towers, I could hear the bass thumping from outside. It was Doug E. Fresh and Slick Rick's "The Show." When we got inside, Gumby and I separated. I'd seen Salaam over in the corner of the room.

"What up. I see ya' finally made it."

"Everybody is lookin' fa' somethin' to smoke. Ya' kno' my homeboys Nick and Darryl, right? They want a li'l somethin'."

"Where they at?"

"Hold up. I'll go get 'em," Salaam said, walking away.

I surveyed the crowd and saw Nadia dancing with this Black dude who was on the basketball team. I could tell by the way he was dancing with her that they were more than dance partners.

"Hello, James," I heard someone say.

I looked down and over my right shoulder and saw Nikki. "Wassup, girl."

"I've been waiting for you to get here."

"Well, I'm here," I said, looking down at her and smiling.

"Ooh! That's my song. Come on, let's dance," she said as E. U.'s "Doin It in the Butt" came on.

Before I could say anything, Salaam was back with Nick and Darryl.

"Not right now. I gotta take care of something."

"Aiight. You owe me a dance," Nikki said, walking away with a slight attitude. She was looking good with some spandex on. Her body was trying to bust out of them spandex.

"Yo, Harris, we want to get a hundred piece from ya'," Darryl said.

"No problem. I'll be back," I said, walking off over to a secluded area where no one paid me any attention and started pulling out twelve dime bags.

I went back over to them, and they gave me the money as I passed them the weed.

"Good lookin'," Darryl said. "Just stick around and you're gonna make a killin'. Everybody in here is lookin' for some weed," Salaam said.

It wasn't even five minutes that passed, and the Jersey crew came to cop some weed. Then the females started coming over getting some too. That's when all the attention was on me. Nikki and her crew of fraternity girls were watching when this White girl from Hartford, Connecticut, named Robin came over to me and started talking to me.

"Hey, James. I see you playing today. I didn't know you was a quarterback."

"Yeah. I just need more playing time."

"Don't worry. You'll get it. I wanted to ask you if you got some smoke."

"Yeah."

"I want to get some, but I don't have the money on me right now. But I'll pay you later."

"No swear. What you want?"

"What you got?"

"Hold up," I said quickly pulling out two bags. "It's some good shit."

"Coming from you, of course. See ya' later," she said, walking away.

I could feel Nikki's eyes on me, but I didn't look in her direction as more people were approaching me.

By midnight, I was almost out of weed, and the party was far from over. The deejay was just starting to crank it up with their hometown favorite, Schooley Dee. Salaam and I seemed like the only guys not dancing. Then I felt someone tapping me on the shoulder.

"Girl…you try'na sneak up on me."

Robin started laughing, and I could see she was feeling good.

"Nooo. I just wanted to know if you had some more. My friends wanted to buy some, so I came over here to ask you."

Salaam was ear hustling and said, "Who's ya' friends?"

"Come on. I'll show you them," she said, leading the way.

We followed her and I couldn't help but notice this White girl was built like a goddess. She had a nice tan that accentuated her facial features, and when she smiled, she had even pearly whites. We got over by her friends, and she introduced us to three White girls who were all brunettes just like her. I gave her the weed, and she passed it to one of the girls and then came over and stood by my side while Salaam socialized with her friends.

"Do you smoke?"

"Nah, I'm a square," I said.

"Yeah right," she said.

I looked out into the crowd and saw Nikki dancing with her girlfriends and looking directly at me. I wasn't doing nothing but talking but felt uncomfortable because my mind was thinking about doing something that I might regret later.

"What's wrong?"

"We got some admirers," I said.

Robin looked in Nikki's direction and turned her back toward me and said, "You wanna go someplace else where it's comfortable?"

"Yeah, but hold up," I said, walking over to where Salaam was at. "Yo, Salaam. Do you have a spot I can go lay low wit' this girl?"

"Just go upstairs. Ask Nick for the key. Don't stay all night. I'm try'na bring somebody up for a quick booty call too."

On that note, I went and found Nick. He was in the corner with two girls from the track team. I told him I needed the key for the room, and he accommodated. Me. I went back over to Robin. She was with her friends and Salaam.

I walked right up on her and passed her the key without anybody noticing. "Go upstairs. I'm right behind you. The last door to the right," I said, remembering Nick's comment.

I talked with Salaam and the girls for about ten minutes before I went upstairs. I made it up to the room without being noticed and knocked on the door.

Robin opened it immediately and said, "What took you so long?"

"I had to play it off. I don't want nobody following me up here."

I could see in Robin's eyes that she was ready for whatever, so I went and sat on the bed. She followed me and sat beside me.

Then she started rubbing her hands between my thighs and said, "You know what I want to do?"

I looked in her hazel eyes with a smirk on my face and said, "What?" I was getting good and stiff.

It was starting to feel good and then I heard a loud knock on the door.

"Yeah," I said as Robin kept hard at work.

"Open up the damn door, James. I know that bitch is in there with you."

I thought it was Nick or Salaam wanting to come in, but it was Nikki. Robin had stopped what she was doing and looked petrified. I could hear Nikki's friends out there too.

"Oh my god. They're going to kick my ass," Robin whispered.

"No, they're not. I won't let them do that," I said, wondering how I would stop them from doing that if they wanted to.

"Hide under the bed," I said to Robin.

When she was under the bed, I opened the door. Nikki and two of her girlfriends named Dee Dee and Pam was with her.

"Where's that bitch? I know she's in here."

"Who are you talking about?" I said, standing by the door.

"Let me in," Nikki said trying to push me out of the way.

"This ain't my room so don't be touching nothing."

"Come on, girl. Forget about her," Pam said.

"I know that White bitch is in there, and if I see her around you, I'm gonna fuck her up," Nikki said, leaving with her friends.

I looked at them leaving and went back in the room. Robin came from under the bed and was shook up. Needless to say, my classic blowjob was blown over by the interruption.

The following weeks went smoothly with the weed. I sold my weight and got another fifty pounds. The Mexican wanted to front me another fifty pounds, but I didn't want it because I didn't plan on selling weed for a long time. I went and bought a black Cherokee Jeep to get around Philly.

The football season was about to end. Our record was 6–4 with one game left against Rutgers. Nikki and I had grown closer to each other and was seeing each other on a regular basis despite the homecoming incident.

For the thanksgiving holiday, I went to her house in Trenton, New Jersey, to meet her family. She drove the Jeep to Jersey that Thanksgiving morning. We got there just before eleven, and her house was already filled with relatives. I left out of the dining room after meeting her first cousin named Duke, who was around my age, along with her uncles and went into the kitchen to meet her mother.

"Mom. This is James. My boyfriend I've been telling you about."

"Nice to meet you, Ms. Brown."

"I hope y'all hungry because we got a lot of food and dinner will be ready in a half hour," Ms. Brown said, walking away to check the turkey in the oven.

Nikki looked like a younger version of her mom. She was very well-proportioned and not overweight. I could see how Nikki would look ten or even thirty years from now.

"You can go in the living room with my cousin and uncles. I know you want to watch college football."

"Nice meeting y'all," I said to her aunts and her cousin, Shanice, who was Duke's younger sister.

I went in the living room and walked right into the middle of them talking about Mike Tyson.

"I know that Iron Mike will be the champion for a long time. He's young and invincible," Duke said.

"Man, Trevor Berbick ain't nobody. Wait till he has to fight Larry Holmes," one of Nikki's uncles said.

"Man, Larry Holmes is too old. Ain't he?" Duke said, looking my way.

"Yeah. Mike Tyson is on a mission," I said.

Duke looked at me and smiled. Then kept on getting his point across by emphasizing how powerful and intimidating Tyson is in the ring.

Nikki's mother cut the debate short by calling everyone to come eat. The table was laid out with the traditional turkey and cranberry, stuffing, and macaroni and cheese. The other side dishes were green beans, mashed potatoes, and sweet potato pie. We all sat and ate at the table, but no one waited for the other person. I sat between Nikki and her mother and enjoyed the good and conversation.

I went in the living room when they got cleaned up, and Duke asked me if I wanted a drink.

"What ya' got?"

"Jack Daniels and some beer."

"Give me some Jack," I said.

We started drinking and conversing. I found out that Duke was hustling in Trenton.

I could look and tell that he wasn't doing it big, so I asked him, "If you had access to a lot of work, how much you think you could move in a week?"

"About two bricks," Duke said without smiling.

That was all I needed to hear. I got Duke's number and told him I'll hook up with him real soon.

When Nikki and I got back to Philly, I went to the dorms and found Salaam in a room, gambling with the basketball players.

When he got off the dice, I said, "Whassup, Salaam, I need to kick it wit' ya'."

He looked at my face and saw that I was serious. "I'll be back in one sec."

"Nah, fuck that. You got all the money," a guy shouted from the game.

Salaam ignored him and said, "You kno' where to get some snow?"

Salaam looked at me for a while before he answered, "Yeah. How much ya' talkin' bout?"

"Two birds."

"I can hook ya' up," Salaam said, playing with his mustache. A habit I noticed he did when he was thinking. "When do you want to do this?"

"Next week," I said.

"Aiight. Next Friday," Salaam said, giving me his hand to shake on it. "Let me get back to the game," he said.

The following Friday, we took a cab over to Germantown to meet the Mexican man. There weren't that many people on the street because it was cold outside. We walked down the block after getting out the cab to a house with a big maple tree in the yard.

Salaam rang the bell, and the Mexican man came to the door. "*Que pasa*, Mr. Ruiz?"

"What's goin' on, Salaam? Come inside. It's cold out there," Mr. Ruiz said, closing the door then leading the way to a room that looked like his living room. "Have a seat," he said, pointing to a leather sofa.

"You remember what I was talking to you about the other day? Well, this is the man that want to do business wit' ya'."

Mr. Ruiz looked at me and nodded his head. "Ya' name is Harris?"

"Yeah," I said.

"Whatta yo' want?"

"Well, I would like to get two birds, but I gotta kno' ya' price."

"Well, I can give it to ya' for thirty-two gees."

When I heard the price, I knew I had to jump on it. I had forty grand in my pocket. "I'll take it," I said, going in my pocket and pulling out my bankroll.

Mr. Ruiz looked at me and said, "*Una momento*. I need ya' word that you'll only deal wit' me."

I looked at this short stocky man and saw that he was serious. "Ya' got my word, Mr. Ruiz."

The following weeks that led toward Christmas was a blur. I got Nikki to find us an apartment, which she did on Broad and Girard. It was a two-room apartment with a kitchen and bathroom. It sat right above from Kentucky Fried Chicken. I furnished the apartment in a week. It had two girls that lived right above us that were roommates who were attending Temple too. More on them later.

I mailed money home through Western Union to Michelle for my son to have Christmas presents and stayed in Philly while winter recess was in progress. I kept the weed in my dorm room and the cocaine in my apartment. Salaam and I were in the weed business. I was traveling to Trenton on a regular basis.

When my classes started back up in January, I was still going to Trenton. I would come back early in the morning just in time for class.

It was late in January on a Friday morning around 4:00 a.m. when I came home, and Nikki was still up when I opened the door to the apartment. She was lying down on the sofa with the television still on.

"Why are you still up?"

"I couldn't sleep. I was worrying about you."

"You ain't been worrying before."

"Well…I wasn't pregnant before."

I sat down by her leg on the sofa and started rubbing her ass while she laid there with one of my Temple T-shirts on. "Are you sure?"

"Of course, I'm sure," she said, looking back at me and rolling her eyes. "And it's yours."

"It better be," I said. "How long you knew this?"

"I just found out yesterday. I'm only five weeks."

"Okay. I'm tired. Can we go to bed?" I said, standing up and yawning.

"We'll talk about this later?"

"Yeah," I said, heading to the bedroom.

From then on, I started hustling harder and spending less money. I had some Italian boys who were attending Temple and buying a half of bird from me every week. They were from West Oakland but stayed in the dorm. They were part of a fraternity. This made me raise my re-up to four birds because I now had from Temple Hospital up to Thirteenth Street with the help of Salaam, Nick, and Darryl. They were all involved in some neighborhood group homes. This made them look respectful and responsible.

One cold day in March, I went to the dorm early on a Friday night with Nelson and Vick who were on the football team. We were coming from Eddie's Bar. There was nobody in there, so we decided to finish drinking at the dorm. When we go there, Nikki was in her room balled up in the bed when I stopped to get some money.

She looked up at me and said, "I didn't expect you to come here."

"It's cold out thurr, so me and the boys came back to kick it in the dorms. Why you're not home?"

"I'm too tired right now."

"Are you aight?"

"Yeah. I'm just tired."

"Well…I'll be in Vick's room," I said, leaving out.

We were drinking Jack Daniels and apple juice, a.k.a. apple jack, and kicking it for a while when Leslie Shepard came barging through the door.

"Yo, Harris! Nicole needs you to come to her room right now."

"Aiight," I said, standing up and feeling tipsy.

"You want us to come?" Vick said.

"Nah," I said, walking toward the door.

When I got to her room, Nikki was still in bed in the fetal position. I saw the sheets stained with blood and started getting scared.

"James. Help me," she said, crying.

"What's wrong?" I asked, running to her side.

"I don't know. I'm too scared to move. I got up to use the bathroom and started bleeding, so I opened the door and seen your teammate and told him to get you. It was an emergency."

"Aiight. I gotta get ya' to the hospital," I said, looking for her coat.

I ran out the room and went to go get Vick and Nelson. I told them what happened and gave Vick the keys to my Jeep and told him to go start it up. I told Nelson to come help me with Nikki. We got back to the room, and he grabbed her coat and her MCM bag with her ID while I carried her to the Jeep. We drove to Temple Hospital and went straight to the emergency room where the nurses took over. One nurse came back and told me that it was a miscarriage, and the doctor would let me see her in a little while.

When I finally went in to see Nikki, she looked pale.

"Can I take her home?"

"You can but she must rest and don't let her do anything strenuous for a while," the doctor said.

I drove Nelson and Vick back to the dorms and took Nikki to our home. It was freezing outside as I carried her from the Jeep to the apartment. We got inside and got comfortable right on the sofa. I placed her head on my lap and stroked her forehead.

"Thank you for being there. I was scared."

"That's why I'm here."

"I know. Do you still love me?" Nikki asked, looking up at me.

"I'll never stop," I said, looking into her brown but swollen eyes.

"I just wish that… Never mind."

"You just wish what?"

"I just wish that wouldn't have happened. I really wanted a part of you to be with me forever."

"I'm not going nowhere. Stop trippin'," I said, looking at her crying.

We stayed up talking until the break of dawn. This incident brought us closer together than ever before. I had stopped hustling for two months. Then I got tired of not having whatever I wanted. Besides, Duke was ringing my phone off the hook to crank it back up in Jersey.

The summer came and I didn't go back home. I stayed in Philly and hustled. Nikki and I went everywhere—Atlantic City, New York City, Great Adventure, and Kings Dominion. Duke and I even hung out together. He took me clubbing to New York at the Latin Quarters. He took me to club Zanzibar in Newark too.

School was about to start back when Salaam and I were walking in King Prussia Mall and ran into this girl I used to see in school.

"Hey, James," she said, walking toward us chewing on some gum.

"How ya' doin'?" I said, not remembering her name.

"Whassup, Bonnie."

"Where I know you from?"

"Public speaking class," Salaam said.

"Yeah! That's right. What are y'all doing out here?"

"Same thing you're doin'," I said.

"Excuse me, Mr. Football."

I looked at Bonnie and started smiling. She had charisma, and I knew I had to get to know her better.

"Pardon my sarcasm," I said, stepping closer to her.

Salaam knew this was his cue to keep it moving and slowly started walking away.

"You live out this way?"

"No. I'm from North Philly. What are you doing back in Philly? School doesn't start for another couple of weeks."

"Yeah, but the football team must be ready early. What ya' got planned for the weekend?"

"Nothing in particular."

"I would like to take you out. You got a number I can call?"

"Yeah… Hold up," Bonnie said, putting her bags down and opening her MCM purse to retrieve a pen and a piece of paper. "Here you go."

"I'll call ya' tomorrow and we'll talk."

"Sounds good, but what do you know about Philly?"

"Don't sleep on me. I'll surprise you."

"How do you know I like surprises?" she said smiling.

I looked at Bonnie and sized her up. She was high-maintenance with jewelry, a Anita Baker hairdo, and Guess all the way down. She probably had a man.

"You like my surprises," I said, giving her my million-dollar smile and walking away to catch up to Salaam.

The next day when I came home from Jersey, I threw eighty thousand dollars on the bed wrapped up in rubber bands inside a Footlocker bag.

"Hey, Nikki, I'm fid'na go out wit' my boys!" I yelled.

She came in the bedroom and said, "What I'm supposed to do?"

"You got friends. Go hang out wit' cha girls."

"Well, don't ask me where I've been when you come home and I'm not here," she said with an attitude.

I didn't even respond to the comment. I was tired of being smothered by her. I needed space. Ever since her miscarriage, our relationship has been too much pressure on me. She was throwing the incident in my face as if it was my fault.

I showered and left out the crib dressed in silk and some Johnston & Murphys on my feet. When I pulled up on Bonnie's block, she was standing outside. She was looking even better than the day before with a body-hugging dress on. I got out the Jeep and opened the passenger side for her to get in and got a whiff of her perfume.

"You look good," I said.

"You don't look bad yourself," she said.

We got in the Jeep, and I pulled off with Anita Baker playing. I had my sound system put in down in New York City on Canal Street, a spot Duke put me up on. We rode in silence and let Anita Baker do all the talking.

I took her to a down-low Italian restaurant in downtown Philly that Salaam hipped me to. I could tell she was impressed; our conversation came easy. I ate veal and she baked ziti. We drank some red wine and got loose with the tongue.

"I like the way you sound."

"What cha mean, girl?"

"You sound country," Bonnie said laughing.

"You talk like a White girl."

"No, I don't!" she said, giggling through her sips of wine.

"Yeah, you do."

"Well, I don't fuck like one."

"How would I know? I haven't fucked ya' and don't wanna."

"You don't, huh?"

"Nope. I want to make love to ya'."

"You do, huh? You think you're ready for this?"

"I'm fit'na find out," I said, smiling and looking right in her eyes to let her know I was serious.

After we ate, we went to Eddie's Bar and drank some more. I could really see me being with Bonnie. I was really feeling her energy. It was two in the morning when we left Eddie's. I drove Bonnie home and kissed her good night.

When I got home, I was horny as the devil. I went into the bedroom and saw Nikki and knew I had to have her. I could tell she wasn't sleeping because she moved over. I started kissing her neck and grinding on her ass until she reciprocated.

"Stop, James."

"Why?"

"Because…I'm…not…messing…with you tonight."

"Aight," I said, continuing my antics until she gave in, and I slid it in from behind.

Soon, I had Nikki's legs cocked in the air and was deep inside her womb. It was feeling good. Makeup sex always feels good; I guess the emotions affect the spirit and make the orgasm more intense. We came at the same time and then fell asleep with me still inside her.

Chapter 3

Life of a Player

It is easier to cope with a bad conscience than with a bad reputation.

—Friedrich Nietzsche

During my sophomore year, I had a plan. I wasn't going to play second fiddle to Anthony Richardson at quarterback, so I told Coach Aarons to let me play wide receiver. He's seen my work at practice against the defensive backs and was willing to give it a try.

My first game as wideout was the homecoming game against East Carolina. Pretty Tony threw a twenty-yard touchdown to me. I was a good compliment to Leslie Shepard, who was the other wideout with four-four speed. I had four-five speed, but my height made me a hard match for defensive backs. I was keeping the double team off Shepard. I was a major player on the team.

Nikki and I were back on good terms, but it wasn't going to last long because Bonnie was the one for me, even though I'd started messing with girls from other colleges. Yvette from Penn State was a fine-ass redbone, Candance from Drexel was a tall blond, and Shannon from Villanova was the finest of them all. She was built like a mature woman but was only nineteen. She had a mocha complexion with long legs. I swear her nipples could get half-inch long when she was aroused.

Math was the last class I had before my midterm break, and I was glad. I left class with my thoughts going to hustling. I jumped in the white Pathfinder I'd just bought a few weeks ago and went to Jersey. This was one of my regular habits now. Sometimes I would leave practice and come straight out here to check on Duke. I pulled up in front of his house and saw his black 3-Series Beemer and knew he was home. I rang the doorbell, and he came to the door in Sergio Tachinni sweat suit and no shirt on.

"Come in, homeboy. I was just about to call ya'."

"Yeah. Whassup?"

"I jus' need some work, mo' work," Duke said, sitting down in front of stacks of money with rubber bands around them.

He gave me ten stacks. I knew each was ten gees. It was after four.

I knew I would make it back in time with work for Duke, so I said, "I'm fit'na take care of business and come check for ya' tomorrow."

"Damn! Aiight, come early," Duke said, getting up and walking me to the door.

On Fridays, I didn't have class, so I took care of business and was home by 9:00 p.m. because I had football practice the next day. I had just finished eating some KFC when Nikki came home.

"What are you doing home so early?"

"I got practice in the morning."

"That never stopped you from hanging out before. I guess dogs get tired too."

Now I knew we had our ups and downs, but this bitch was getting out of hand.

"Who you callin' a dog?"

"James, I seen you with that bitch yesterday. You come in late last night and was sleeping hard this morning, so I didn't want to wake you and say nothing." She was talking about Shannon from Villanova. I ate lunch with her downtown.

"I can't have girls for friends now, huh?"

"Y'all looked like more than friends. James…I'm not dumb."

I saw an argument coming and wasn't in the mood for it. As Nikki's mouth kept on moving, I got dressed. I would come back later and sleep on the couch.

As I left the apartment and was about to get on the elevator, I heard music coming from upstairs. I decided to go investigate. I went up their flights of stairs and heard the music coming from the apartment that Sonia and Crystal stayed at, so I knocked on the door.

Pretty Tony opened the door. "What up, Harris! We were wondering was you comin'."

"We," I said, walking inside and seeing everybody from the football and basketball team up in there.

Sonia and Crystal were on the track team so most of the girls were from the team. There was plenty of food and alcohol, and I felt right in place with all my boys from the team there. They all thought I was fucking one of the girls, if not both. But to tell you the truth, I wasn't even thinking about them until now. We had walked home from school a couple of times, but it was nothing but small talk about school events.

The party slowed down after 1:00 a.m. and everybody started leaving. Crystal left out with some of the track team and left Sonia and me alone to clean up the mess. Well, I could have left but I didn't.

I moved the furniture back in its proper place then sat on the sofa feeling exhausted.

"I'll be back," Sonia said, going into her bedroom.

I looked around and saw that there was some more alcohol and grabbed a bottle of dark Bacardi and started drinking when Sonia came back into the room wearing a satin red negligee that came down to her thighs.

Now picture this: Sonia has the darkest, smoothest skin I've ever seen. And her legs are very well-defined from running track. The red negligee complimented her skin tone to the fullest.

"I see you're still tryin' to party," she said.

"Can't let good alcohol go to waste," I said.

Not to be outdone, Sonia got a cup, poured some vodka and grapefruit juice in it, and sat on the sofa with me. "Do you still mess with Nicole?"

"Nah. Me and Nikki just live together."

"I'm talkin' 'bout…"

"Same person, her nickname is Nikki."

"My bad for not knowing," Sonia said, getting up to fill her cup again.

We sat and talked for an hour about Nikki, me, her, and school. Then I wanted to lay down because I was drunk.

"What time is it?"

"It's almost five," she said.

I got off the sofa and lay on the carpet. I closed my eyes to stop everything from spinning.

"What's wrong?"

"I'm fucked up," I said. "And I got practice at nine."

"Well, let me make a bed for you," she said, running off to get some blankets and a pillow.

After getting me comfortable, I lay back with my head swaying.

"Ahh, look at the baby," Sonia said, kneeling down, rubbing my forehead.

I just smiled with my eyes closed for a while until I felt her kissing my forehead and cheeks. I opened my eyes and grabbed Sonia by her ass and started tonguing her down. I realized that she didn't have nothing on under the negligee and started sticking a couple of fingers inside her. Before I realized it, Sonia had my jeans loose and was pulling them off. I just took one leg out, and she sat on top of me.

"Ooh, James… You just don't know how long I wanted you to do this," she said while going up and down.

I couldn't believe how much pussy control she had. She was squeezing my dick with her walls and going up and down real slow. When she was about to cum, I could feel her walls tighten even more. Her stamina was incredible because she kept riding me. We kept it at it until six in the morning. Then I got a couple hours of sleep before going home to shower for football practice.

Football season was over, but basketball season was in full stride. Temple wasn't known for their football team, which is another story. Salaam and I fell into the gym for the games and sat in our usual spot with the football players and track team. Sonia came in with the rest of the track team while we were kicking back and listening to Big Alfonso jonesing on Pretty Tony. She came back and squeezed right between Salaam and I and sat down.

"Whassup, baller."

"Whassup, shorty," I said, smiling down at her fine ass.

The basketball team came out and started warming up. Mark Macon and D. Hodge were the two best players on the team.

"Y'all betta' bus' tha' ass!" Alfonso yelled out to the team.

"Don't worry yo. We got 'em!" D. Hodge yelled back.

As they kept warming up, Sonia got up and said, "I'm going to go get some popcorn. You want anything?"

"Yeah. Bring me some back," I said, digging in my pockets.

"I got you, baller," she said, running off to catch her girlfriends.

"Man, stop frontin'. You fuckin' her, Harris," Leslie said.

"If you say so but I ain't," I said with a serious face.

"Well, I would. Fa' rea' she has the baddest body on the campus," Gumby said.

I must admit, he was telling the truth. Sonia had a body women from the motherland have. It was her genetics…and her skin. "Black don't crack," my mother used to always say.

That Saturday night, we went out clubbing after Temple beat Villanova. The manager kept a section reserved for us in VIP because I knew him from when I first started hustling. We had a buffet with buffalo wings, shrimp, burgers, hot dogs, champagne, beer, and alcohol.

I was sitting back and enjoying myself as everyone was partying and bullshitting when Gumby rolled up on me and said, "Yo, Harris, the manager said we're short two yards on this buffet."

"Hold up," I said, digging in my pocket and pulling out a knot. I peeled four fifty-dollar bills and gave them to Gumby, and Sonia was looking from across the table.

I drove Sonia, Crystal, and her man Darnell home.

When we got inside the building, Sonia said, "It's only two. You can come up for a little while."

I thought about Nikki and accepted Sonia's offer.

When we got inside the apartment, Crystal said, "I'm going to bed y'all."

"Aiight. Good night," I said, eyeing Crystal's fat ass in the jeans she was wearing.

Crystal was built similar to Sonia. Just that she was a redbone and kept plenty of men chasing her. I even heard her call them her sponsors. Darnell, who was from DC, was a major player and baller. Crystal lived by the Janet Jackson motto, "What have you done for me lately?" I was caught off guard by Sonia's voice, and for a second, I thought she was going to say something to me about looking at Crystal.

"James, when you were out with your friends, why you're always paying for everything?"

I looked at Sonia and yawned before saying, "I got a lot of money from agents. They know I'm going pro and want to have me as a client."

"Well, everybody says you and Salaam are the weed men."

"Who, me? Nah. Maybe Salaam is doin' somethin'," I said, stretching out on the sofa.

"You are staying here?"

"Yeah, I'll leave in the morning," I said, kicking off my shoes and getting comfortable.

Sonia went in the closet to get some blankets and said, "Come lay down here with me."

I got under the blankets with her, and after a while, I was inside her.

*****

Spring came back quickly but not as quickly as the money came. I bought Nikki a BMW, and she had the nerve to have an attitude. I haven't touched her in over two months and bought her a car. I must be the stupidest man in the world. I just wanted to keep her busy while I was with Bonnie.

Bonnie was another story. She didn't smother me and kept money. Now I'm not the jealous type, but she must have a man other than me because she didn't want for nothing. When the summer came, we were going to Atlantic City just about every other weekend. We would shop till we dropped at the Cherry Hill Mall.

One late July when we were coming from Atlantic City, my beeper was going off like crazy with the 911 code. I knew it had to be Salaam. I hadn't seen him in a week. I dropped Bonnie off at home and went over to his house. He opened the door, and by the look on his face, I knew something was wrong.

"Whassup, cuz," I said.

"Man, Harris. I kno' ya' heard by now."

"Nah. Heard what?" I said, walking behind him into the living room.

He started pacing the floor, so I sat down in the La-Z-Boy.

"I got busted Thursday night. The police pulled me over for not using my signal lights, and I don't have my license. So they searched the ride and found coke inside the car."

"Damn!" I said, upset that I just found out. I let him finish telling me what happened and decided to take a break from hustling in Philly.

"Don't worry, man. I got you if you need anything. You need to cool out for a while and lay low."

Salaam agreed and then told me about the Junior Black Mafia (JBM). The JBM were pressing him to get off Broad and Montgomery. They didn't have to worry about seeing Salaam anymore.

*****

When my junior year started, I had a new plan for being on the team. Leslie Shepard had the wideout spot on lock because he was the go-to man. What the team needed was some help on defense, and I knew I could do that.

One day at practice before a Clemson game, I was looking at Gumby and James Parish doubling up on Alfonso Taylor, who was our best defensive tackle.

I said, "Coach, I could do what Alfonso is doing."

The coach looked back at me and said, "Come on and try it."

I lined up against Gumby and got around him with ease. I did it again. Then I did the same to James Parrish and another offensive tackle named Tre' Johnson.

Coach Aarons had seen enough and said, "This weekend, we play Clemson, and I'm going to start you at defensive end."

Game day came and the weather was sunny and seventy degrees. I had come out on the field on the first series and got a sack on second down, which I shared with Alfonso. By halftime, I had one and a half sacks. The second half was more of the same. We dominated Clemson with our defense. We left South Carolina with a new pride in our defense. I ended the game with two and half sacks.

The following week, Coach Aarons wanted me to start hitting the weights more and eating more protein so that I could get my weight up with more muscle mass. In a month, I had gained nine pounds and weighed 254. This made me change my schedule. I'd stopped husting for a while. But when Duke called me and said it was an emergency, I only messed with him, and of course, I had the weed to sell in my dorm. Since I was in the gym a lot, people would slide by my dorm after 6:00 p.m. to get some weed. Sometimes, I'd stay in the dorm instead of going to the apartment because I didn't want to hear Nikki's mouth, or I would be trying to avoid Sonia.

It was Wednesday that I'd just gotten fifty pounds of weed. I stashed it in my closet and sold five pounds to this Italian kid in my dorm. My roommate was named Parrish Sims. He was a freshman and on the football team too. He'd come in the room about ten minutes after I sold the weed to the Italian kid.

"Whassup, Parrish," I said.

"Nothin' much," he said, throwing his books down on his bed. "I'm starving like Marvin."

"Well, I'm fit'na go out. I'll be back kind of late, but I can bring you back some KFC."

"Sounds like a winner. Ayo, Harris. You smell that?" Parrish said, sniffing the room.

"Smell what?" I said, sniffing too.

"You don't smell that weed?"

I sniffed the air again and then went to the vent and smelled it. "Yeah. Somebody is smoking in their room. It's coming from the vent," I said, thinking nothing of it and leaving.

I went to check on Duke in Jersey and got back to the dorm around nine o'clock that night and couldn't believe what I saw when I went up to my room. The school police were up in my room. They had my roommate sitting on the floor in the hallway and was bringing out the suitcase with the weed in it. I knew I had a decision to make, and I'd made up my mind. I told the officers it was mine, and my roommate wasn't aware of it being in the room. To my surprise, I wasn't arrested but was taken to the dean the next morning by the school police. Coach Aarons was right beside the dean.

The dean looked at me when I entered the office and said, "Have a seat, Mr. Harris."

I looked at Coach Aarons, who said nothing but gave me an assuring nod with his head to sit down.

"I don't know what you were thinking but we do not tolerate drugs on this campus. Not even alcohol. Your coach here says you are a good player, and looking at your school record, you have a *B* average. I must say that is good for an athlete on a scholarship. I don't want to kick you off the team and ruin your future before it gets started, so I'm going to kick you off campus. You can attend your classes and still play football, but if I hear of another incident with your name, you will be expelled."

I looked at the dean and said, "Thank you, sir. And I understand." I then left the office.

I looked at that as a blessing because I could've easily gotten a federal charge. It didn't stop me from hustling. What it did do was help me be more careful in how I conducted my illegal business. I did step my football game up too. The next following games, I played like I was possessed. In a game against Pittsburg, I sacked the quarterback three times. In another game against Penn State, I broke Bobby Johnson's leg on a reversed kickoff they tried to pull on our special teams. By the end of October, I was second in punt and field goal blocking in the NCAA division. I made the All-American team and fooled the critics again. They'd said I'd never make it. Even though we didn't have a bowl bid, it was a good year for me.

When Thanksgiving came around, Nikki went to visit her family, but I didn't go. Nine months had passed since I had sex with her. I spent Thanksgiving with Sonia and Bonnie. I went to Bonnie's apartment first then spent the rest of the night with Sonia. Crystal came back home with one of her sponsors just when Sofia and I were getting comfortable.

So I said, "Let's go down to my apartment."

"You sure? What about Nicole?"

"She's at her people's house in Jersey," I said, assuring her that it was all right.

Crystal and her sponsor saw us getting off the sofa, and Crystal said, "Where are y'all goin'? You don't have to leave on account of us."

"We aiight. We just goin' down to my spot," I said.

We got down to my apartment, and Sonia said, "Hmm, you livin' large," while staring at the furniture. "Damn! We got the same exact apartment, but the furniture makes yours look different."

"You want something to drink?" I asked, going in the cabinet and pulling out a bottle of Smirnoff Vodka.

"Yeah. You got some grapefruit juice?"

"Of course. Just sit back and act like you're upstairs," I said, pouring her a drink and making me one too.

She turned on the television set to Arsenio Hall, and we sat down and got comfortable on the sofa, drinking and laughing, when Nikki came through the door with her man named Kevin.

"What are you doin' here?" I spoke.

"What, you mad? You need to go," she said.

Sonia was about to get up, and I grabbed her arm, and she sat back down.

"You told me you weren't coming back today."

"Can we go to the kitchen and talk?" Nikki said.

Nikki led the way as I went in the kitchen and started arguing with her. I eventually won the verbal dispute in, say, five minutes by unanimous decision. She left out the apartment upset and slammed the door.

"Damn! How can you live with each other? It's too much hostility between y'all," Sonia said, sipping her drink.

"We have different schedules," I said, sitting down next to her.

We caught the last ending of *Arsenio Hall Show* and made our way down on the carpet from kissing to the sixty-nine position. The one thing I like about Sonia is that she was on birth control, so I had the pleasure of feeling and filling her womb. I hated using condoms.

When Christmas came around, football season was over. I couldn't put up with Nikki's bullshit anymore, so I told Bonnie to find an apartment. I stayed in Philly for the holidays and sent money through Western Union back home to Michelle and my son.

It was two days into the New Year, 1991, and I decided to go hang out by myself. I went to this strip club called Knights on Broadway. I didn't want to be around Sonia or Bonnie because I was depressed. I could feel that my life needed a change. I was ready to get out of Philly too.

When I entered Knights on Broadway, I sat in my usual spot which was in the corner and off to the side. There were three sisters who were strippers in the club that I knew very well. Janette, a.k.a. Lady, who I messed with a few times, and her sisters Star and Angel. They knew all in the club and put on a lesbian show on the stage. Janette had a banana in her pussy while Star ate part of it that was sticking out. Angel sprayed whipping cream on Star's ass cheeks and licked it all off while Star and Janette were doing their thing. I was getting horny just watching them as Janette looked right over at me in the corner. I got up from my spot and went to ask the manager for the keys to the basement.

Big Ed looked at me and said, "You want a personal sho'?"

"Here ya' go," I said, going into my pocket and pulling out two fifties. "I won't be long."

"Take as long as want," Big Ed said, giving me the keys.

I went and got Lady, and to my surprise, Star and Angel asked if they could come.

I looked at both and smiled. "Yeah. Y'all can come."

We didn't waste no time once we got down in the basement and locked the door. Their outfits came off right away. I bent Lady and

Star over some beer boxes and had double the pleasure of Black flesh spread out in front of me. I didn't know where to start. I figured I'd start with Lady first. She was already wet. I just ended up fucking them both by dipping in one and then taking it out and putting it in the other one. Of course, I had a body bag. Angel was looking at us and started finger fucking herself. When she got tired of that, she came over, got on her knees between my legs, and started sucking my balls. It felt too good, but it wasn't good enough to feel Angel going in my pocket and taking my money.

I grabbed her by her extensions and pulled her head back and said, "Break ya' self an' gimme mine, bitch."

"Whatta' ya' talkin about?"

"Oh! You wanna act stupid?" I said, pulling out of her sister and sticking my hand in her G-string.

Her sisters were looking at me when I pulled her G-string off. I found my knot rolled up stuck inside her pussy. I snatched it out, wiped it off on her legs, and put it in my pocket.

"Let's go," I said.

"Where we goin'?" Lady said.

"We gettin' tha fuck outta here," I said.

"I don't have nothin' to cover me up," Angel said.

"We're in a strip club, bitch. Get outta here," I said, grabbing her by the arm.

I gave Big Ed back his keys and went home. I got inside the apartment and staggered to the bathroom and took a shower. When I came out, I felt a lot better. I went into the bedroom and saw Nikki sleeping. I took off my boxers and got in bed with her. She moved over, so I could get in, and I took it from there. I started sucking on her neck and left a hickey. She turned over for me and kissed me and then got on top of me.

She put it inside her and said, "Hmm, James…that feels good."

I started moving in rhythm with her hops.

"I miss you," she said as we humped away.

We never switched that position. Nikki started crying, and I lifted my upper torso and kissed the tears off her face.

After that night, Nikki and I never had sex again, but we were friends again. When her boyfriend came around, I didn't show no hostility toward him. I even brought beer from the store for me and him to drink while he waited to take Nikki out on a date. That's what Nikki and I needed to get out of the way…one last episode.

In late January, Bonnie found an apartment downtown, and we moved in together. I started hustling hard with Duke again while going to school. Football season was over with, and I was considering entering the draft. I was first defensive of team All-American. I still had some haters who said I wasn't ready for the NFL, so I decided to enter the draft in late February and told Coach Aarons. He wished me luck.

Chapter 4

The Next Level

Many are called but few are chosen.

—Matthew 22:14

I had a lot of loose ends to tie up with Duke in Jersey before I went to the COMBON in Indianapolis to show the scouts my skills. I started staying in Trenton until the break of dawn and drove straight to class from there. I would tell Bonnie where I was, and she understood.

The night before I had to take a flight to Indiana, I helped Duke bag up some bricks that took us six hours to do. I was so tired. I slept the whole plane ride to Indiana. When I got the Grand Hyatt Hotel, I told the desk lady my name and was given a room key. When I got up to the room, there was somebody there. A guy from Michigan State who I remembered playing against.

"Whassup. I didn't kno' you was comin' out this year."

"I had better. This was a good year for me," I said.

"I thought I seen ya' face… You made All-American?"

"Yeah."

"Congratulations. I'm going downstairs to talk to a few of the guys. We'll kick it later."

"Fa' sure," I said as he left the room.

Later on that night when my roommate and I were in the room about to go to sleep, he said, "I'm so excited about tomorrow that I can't sleep."

"Yeah. Everybody is goin' to be there," I said, yawning and trying to give him a hint that I was tired. I fell asleep while he was talking to me.

The next day started early. I had to take a physical and piss test. Then came the tests for strength, endurance, and speed. I entered the gym, where the stage was set to bench-press 225 pounds. A white boy from USC was on the bench and repped it thirty-nine times. I knew that was impressive enough to get the heads of the scouts to acknowledge my presence.

I moved on to run the forty-yard dash. I was running against the clock and was timed at 4.55. I knew that had to be impressive for a defensive lineman who weighed in at 257 pounds. The rest of the day went smooth with my vertical being tested at thirty-eight inches. My height was six feet six inches with eight-foot wingspan.

When the day ended, I went back to the hotel to get ready for the party. I got dressed in the room and was finished before my roommate. I had put on a Hugo Boss suit with a crew neck and some Lorenzo Banfi shoes. My Michigan State roommate wasn't shabby himself. His two-tone Stacey Adams was matching perfectly with his pinstripe suit. I just didn't like the conservative look.

"I like your style," he said, eyeing my clothes.

"Yeah. You're dressed as if it was draft day," I said, making him laugh as we made our way downstairs.

We went to the bar of the Grand Hyatt Regency, and everybody was there. It was wall to wall of agents, scouts, and women, along with college prospects.

"Hey, Harris. I liked your performance today."

I turned around and saw a middle-aged White man who I didn't remember being introduced to.

"My name is John Turling. I'm the defensive line coach for the Vikings."

"How are you doing?" I said, extending my hand to him.

He shook my hand and then my roommate's. He turned his attention back to me and said, "What are you drinking?"

"Whatever…"

"It doesn't matter. Come on with me. I got you," he said, walking over toward the bar.

I followed John and left my roommate behind. John Turling was built like a tank. I could tell in his younger days he was hell on the field. He ordered two beers for us, and we sat at the bar.

"You know, we are looking at building up our defense. I got a lot of say-so. I like what I have seen in you. Would you like to come to Minnesota if I pulled some strings to get you?"

"Yeah, I would like to play for Minnesota."

"Well, we don't have a first round pick because we traded it, but I want you to know that your stock may drop," he said, taking a sip from his beer.

I drank mine and said, "Why?"

"You want another drink?"

"Yeah," I said, still curious as to why he would tell me that my stock had fallen.

I'd been an underdog since I was in high school. Coach Shannon said I wasn't going to make it because I didn't have what it took to play on a collegiate level. Then in college, I had to hear that I was mediocre. I had a tendency of taking some play, so I stepped up my game and became an All-American my junior year, and now I'm hearing my stock dropped.

"You took a urine test, and it came back positive with cocaine in your urine."

I started thinking and was glad when the beers came just before I could respond. I knew I don't use drugs. But just maybe it was when I helped Duke cook up two bricks and bag some rocks up without gloves and a mask on that I got some cocaine in my system.

"I don't care about that. I believe you'll stop using it and step up to the task in the NFL," John Turling said.

I just drank my Michelob and nodded my head as he spoke. John bought another round of beers for us as agents came by to speak to him and me.

I wasn't impressed by none of their sales pitches until one came up to me when John went to the bathroom and said, "Harris? James Harris, right?"

"Yeah," I said, putting my beer down and turning around.

"I'm Harold," he said, passing me a white card with gold-engraved letters on it.

"Hey! What's happening, Hal?" Mr. Turling said, walking up on us.

Harold turned around and extended his hand and said, "How you doing, John? It's been a while. I'm just talking to Mr. Harris about considering me as an agent."

"We, Harris, I can assure you that he's a good agent."

I nodded my head, looked at the card again, and said, "I'll call you and we'll talk."

"Sounds good to me. What y'all are drinking?"

"Beers," Mr. Turling said.

Harold bought six Michelobs. I sat there and listened to them talk about the draft and the NFL.

"I'll make sure to get you to join the NFL players union," Harold said.

"Why is that so important?" I said.

"Because it's an easy ten grand to pick up," Harold said.

After one more round of beers, I gave Harold my home number and went to the bathroom. I ran into a couple of players who said they were headed for the strip club.

I went back over to Mr. Turling and said, "Mr. Turling, I'll see ya' later. I'm going over to the Ponderosa."

"Oh yeah! I'm going there too," Mr. Turling said, getting up from the bar. "Call me John from now on," he said, patting me on the back.

When we got inside the Ponderosa, we sat at the bar in the main room. A large stage running behind the main room and bar enabled every customer to get a good view of the sexy ladies. While the ladies worked the players for the lap dances in VIP, the agents worked the players by passing their cards out with money. An agent named Floyd gave me his card and two gees. He promised me he could get the best contract for me. I took the money and bought a few lap dances in VIP and tipped the girls very well.

After a few Jack Daniels, I was good and drunk but still able to make it back to the hotel room. A couple of sober players drove the drunk players to the hotel.

My flight back to Philly was at 10:30 a.m., so I slept until nine.

When I got back to the apartment, Bonnie was not home. I unpacked my bag and was about to take a shower when the phone rang.

"Hello."

"Harris. Whut up, man."

"Whassup, kinfolk. I just got back."

"Yeah, I kind of figured that. I called earlier. You heard about Bonnie?" Salaam said.

"Nah. What happened?"

"She got arrested in DC."

"How you found out?"

"You kno' Darnell, the dude that's fuckin' wit' Crystal? He stays in DC and told me about it."

"What he tell ya'?"

"She got arrested in the airport. It was in the paper. Have you seen her?"

"Not yet. I'm goin' to call her mom's house. I'll talk to ya' later," I said, hanging up on Salaam.

I called Bonnie's mother, and she told me she wasn't home, so I decided not to leave a message and wait for her to contact me.

I was knocked out on the sofa with the television on when Bonnie came through the door.

"Where you been?" I said, opening my eyes when she closed the door.

"I went to Texas," she said, heading toward the bedroom with her Louis Vuitton bag.

I got up and followed her into the bedroom and said, "Texas! What's out there?"

"I went out there with a couple of friends. I wasn't with no man," she said, taking off her shoes while sitting on the edge of the bed.

Bonnie never looked at me as of yet since she came through the door; she just kept her head down.

"Don't you have something to tell me?" I said, looking down at her.

"I swear I wasn't with no man," she said, looking up at me.

"Bonnie…don't you think I have enough friends that's gonna tell me when my gets arrested?"

Bonnie looked up into my eyes for the first time, and I saw tears in her eyes. "I'm sorry, James, but I'm scared to tell you what happened.

"Why?" I said, kneeling down and holding her hands.

"Because…because I don't want to get hurt and go to jail," she said, crying.

I grabbed Bonnie and consoled her in my arms. "Everything's gonna be aiight."

"I'm scared," she said, breaking down even more in my arms.

"Scared of what? Tell me what's goin' on," I said, kissing the tears off her cheeks.

Bonnie got her composure and told me how her girlfriend, Deanna, got a Jamaican boyfriend named Trent who had a grocery store. He was selling weed out of it and would give Dee a lot of weed, and they would smoke some and sell some of it. As his clientele grew, Dee would fly to Texas and bring it back for him, and he would pay her a gee. Dee got pregnant, and Bonnie started making the trip with Dee, and they would split the gee and keep some of the weed for themselves. On the previous trip, Dee had a baby boy, so Bonnie made the trip by herself. She followed her regular patter and got off in DC, where she would meet a dude named Nigel but was picked up at the luggage claim by the special task force. They took her back to a room and asked to search her bag and found one hundred pounds of Mexican weed. Dee came and bonded her out of jail. Bonnie hadn't told her mother what happened as of yet.

"Don't worry. I'm gonna get'cha a lawyer."

"I don't wanna go to jail."

"You won't. Not if I can help it," I said, rocking her back and forth in my arms while still on my knees.

The following weeks were busy for me. I gave Bonnie my undivided attention. I'd stop hustling completely now that I knew I was headed to the pros. I got a lawyer for Bonnie and went to court with her in DC. It was back and forth and forth and back from DC to Philly because she was pleading guilty and wanted to get it over with as fast as possible.

When draft day came on the last Saturday of April, we were in the apartment lying on the bed. I turned the television on the draft and caught the beginning. The first person to be picked was Russell Maryland. He was from Miami, Florida, and was going to the Dallas Cowboys. The next five players were all defensive players too. Eric Turner, Bruce Pickens, Mike Croel, Todd Lyght, and Eric Swann. I watched the first round and most of the second until Bonnie finished cooking breakfast for us. We then made love, fell asleep, and was awakened by the phone.

"Hello," I said, yawning.

"Mr. Harris?"

"Speaking."

"This is Mr. Lewis. Congratulations."

"On what?"

"You don't know? You were picked by the Seattle Seahawks in the third round. You slipped a little because…well, you know why."

"Oh, yeah. I fell asleep on the draft."

"Well, I'm here to let you know and help you. I can arrange everything. That's my job."

"Aiight then," I said, looking at Bonnie, who was awake now. "I'll talk to you later," I said before hanging up.

"Who was that?"

"My agent. The Seattle Seahawks drafted me."

"That's great," she said, not too enthused.

I knew Bonnie was worried that I would leave her by herself to deal with her situation. To tell you the truth, I loved Bonnie and would never have considered that.

I got up and put the radio on Power 99. They were playing "Forever My Lady" by Jodeci. I walked back over to the bed, and Bonnie sat up on the pillows.

"I was thinking."

"Thinking about what?" she said.

"'Bout us. Would you marry me?"

"Of course I would," she said with a glint in her eyes that let me know she was excited.

"Come on, let's get dressed."

"Where we going?"

"I'll show you when we get there," I said, heading for the bathroom.

We got dressed and went to eat at a soul food restaurant and sat in the corner, where Bonnie admired her ring I'd just bought through the entire meal.

Before we got back to the apartment, I stopped and bought a bottle of Don Perignon to celebrate with. We didn't get all the way in the crib before we were kissing and groping each other.

"I guess you like the ring."

"It's aiight," she said, trying to sound all nonchalant.

"It's aiight, huh?"

"Yeah," she said, smiling.

"It's aiight," I said, palming her pussy and kissing her.

Bonnie let out a moan and then stuck her tongue in my mouth and grabbed my dick and started rubbing on it like a genie's lamp. The more she rubbed, the more my tongue explored her mouth. She pulled away and started unzipping her jeans. I followed her lead until we were both in our birthday suits.

"How much do you love me?"

"Is that a trick question," I said, holding the champagne in my right hand.

"No. Just answer it, James."

I stood there with my dick hard, staring at Bonnie. I opened the bottle and took a sip.

"Well…"

"Well what?"

"How much do you love me?"

"There's nothin' in this world I can compare it to. It's infinite," I said, taking a sip from the bottle.

"James. I love you," Bonnie said, bending down in front of me and putting my hardness in her mouth.

I stood there drinking champagne and watching Bonnie go to work. I could see she was into it, and it felt good.

"Hmm. Damn, bonbon," I said as she spat my manhood and deep throated me.

I've gotten my dick sucked many times but not like this. My future wife had me ready to explode already. When she picked up the pace, I erupted and felt her sucking every drop from me. I picked Bonnie up and draped her over my shoulder and headed for the bedroom.

"What are you about to do to me?"

"One treat deserves another," I said, laying her down on the bed.

I got right between her legs and spread her open. Her juices were oozing out as I put my tongue on her clit.

"Uhh!" she groaned.

I licked on her clit and watched her squirm in delight. When I decided to stop after five minutes and eased inside her, I did it slowly. She was so wet and hot I had to pull out because I would've come. I did this for a while until I knew she came again and then I decided to get mine.

"Turn around," I said, pulling out of her and watching her turn that ass around for me to hit doggy style.

I mounted Bonnie and rode her as she threw it back at me. After a while, she collapsed on the bed and let me do all the work. Her head was down in the pillow as I lost control and released my semen inside of her. She turned around, and we cuddled until we fell asleep.

The following weeks were all about Bonnie. I'd gotten her a lawyer, and he said that she would get two years in a work release program. That's when we decided to get married.

I met a guy in Annapolis, Maryland, named Curtis who had married his girl who was also in the work release program. He explained to me where we could go do it and helped me contact a Rev. Woods, who had a license to marry us in Annapolis. It was a small church and quick ceremony with only seven people there to witness it. None were our friends or family.

I would drive from Philly every weekend to pick Bonnie up from her job at a McDonald's restaurant and bring her back the next day for work. On the weekdays, I would park in the parking lot and wait for her breaks just to spend time with her. We were inseparable. The manager even saw that and told me that I could sit inside the restaurant and wait for Bonnie. Sometimes, we would swing a quick episode in the Jeep during her lunch break. Other times, we would talk about our future. With me going to Seattle and her getting off the pill, we wanted to have children.

It was late in May when I had to go to the minicamp in Seattle and leave her behind for a while. As I rode the plane to Seattle, I had my family and old friends on my mind. I needed to go back home and see them.

When I got to the Seattle airport, it was 5:00 p.m. Pacific Time and raining. There was a limousine there to pick me up courtesy of the Seattle Seahawks. I was taken straight to a hotel and told to report to the field at ten in the morning. I had a roommate from DC who was running back. He was on the team a couple years already. I remembered seeing him play.

As I unpacked, he said, "My man, what school you come from?"

"Temple."

"In Philly. Do you kno' D. Hodge?"

"Yeah. He's on the basketball team. That's my man."

"Tell him I said whassup when you holla' at him again."

"Fa' sure," I said, feeling a lot more comfortable because he had broken the ice with that conversation.

The next day, we went to Kirkland, Washington, for minicamp. We started out by stretching and doing basic drills. I showed off my foot speed by running the forty and doing some pass rushing drills. I was looking for Brian Bosworth, but he wasn't around. Minicamp was really for the rookie but some of the veterans showed up too.

The next day was a little more intense. We put on equipment, and I showed them my strength by lifting some weights. I had squatted seven hundred pounds eight times. I could see the coaches were impressed. My physical had gone great too. We had to do all this inside because it rained the whole time while I was in Seattle. The day I was leaving to go back to Philly, it was raining too.

When I got back home, I checked the answering machine, and my agent had left a message stating that it was very important that I get in contact with him, so I called him early the next day before going to see Bonnie.

"Mr. Harris. I'm glad you caught me early," Mr. Lewis said.

"Why? Whassup?"

"Nothing really. I just wanted you to know that you've been traded to the Minnesota Vikings."

"What! I just left Seattle's minicamp."

"I know. While you were there, talks were in the making. Mr. Turling really likes you."

"So what's next?"

"You have to report to Minnesota's minicamp by tomorrow."

"That's short notice."

"I know, but this is the way it goes. I can get a good contract for you because they want you. I'll negotiate that as soon as I get off the phone with you," Mr. Lewis said.

"Well, I'm going to get ready to leave," I said as we both hung up the phone.

I had one thing I had to do before I left for Minnesota. That was to see Bonnie.

*****

I made my way inside and saw her on the register. She must've felt my presence because she turned my way. A smile came across her face that made me happy. I got in her line and waited patiently at the end.

"Hey, James. How did it go?"

"You won't believe this. I must go to Minnesota tomorrow."

"What! What happened?"

"I'll explain it to you on your lunch break. Just give me a big mac, large fries, and a large vanilla milkshake." I went and sat in our usual corner and ate my food.

By two o'clock, the crowd slowed down, and Bonnie took her lunch break. We went to the Jeep, and I explained everything to her.

"I think I'll just sell all the furniture out the apartment because when you're released, I want you to come straight out to Minnesota.

"I hope you do," Bonnie said, looking into my eyes. "I'm goin' to miss you."

"I'll be back," I said, reaching over and kissing her.

That's all it took. We had to swing a quick episode.

Chapter 5

All About the Benjamins

You don't have to be smart to make a lot of money.

—Ted Turner

When I got to Minneapolis the following day, I had to get to the Viking facility for orientation. I was sitting through a bunch of rhetoric when this beautiful Black woman come on stage to speak. She was talking about the pitfalls and traps of gold differs and lawsuits. She called on the rookie on stage and went through a demonstration with him.

"Where are we going?" she said as they were pretending to be on a date.

"Back to my hotel room."

"For what?" she said with a smile on her face.

"For a drink or somethin'," the rookie said.

"Let me tell my girlfriend I'm leaving." She pretended to have walked off and came back and then they pretended to be in a hotel room.

"Do you mind if I get comfortable on your bed?"

"No. As a matter of fact, I'll join you," the rookie said, getting plenty of laughs from the crowd as he unbuttoned his shirt and loosened his tie.

That's when they stopped the scene, and she said, "Thank you for your cooperation. Now I want to know by a show of hands, did I want to have sex?"

Many men in the room said yes and gave reasonable explanations.

"Well, I'm here to tell y'all that if put in a situation like that and the female says stop at any time and you don't, it's considered rape."

"Can we have a real date?" the rookie said who was still on the stage with her.

"Sure. But I need to let you know that I'm HIV positive," she said without laughing and then slowly walked off the stage.

Everybody looked astonished when she said that. Then all the smiles and laughing were replaced with whispers. This lady was beautiful and looked better than the average woman on the street with her branded outfit on. That shit was scary. Just to know that AIDS is that easy to catch.

Since I knew that I made the team, I started looking for a place to live in. I got $100,000 for passing the physical, $200,000 for reporting, and $900,000 for signing. This was a three-year deal with an option that made me a millionaire!

After I found me a condo in Eden Prairie, I went back home to see my family and friends before the season started. I pulled up in front of my mother's house and paid the driver. As I stepped out of the cab, my brother Eric came outside.

"Whassup wit'chu, bro?"

"Ain't shit. Where er'ybody at?"

"Mom's at work. She said you were comin'," Eric said, grabbing one of the two bags I had.

"Well, I had to. The season fid'na start," I said, entering the house.

It still looked the same besides the new television and stereo set in the living room.

"You talk to Dad yet?"

"Nah. Mom ain't talk to him lately?"

"No question he knows. He boastin' 'bout ya' in LA. Uncle Junebug jus' got back from out there las' weekend."

"Yeah. What you been up to?" I said, sitting down on the sofa.

"Same ole shit. I been workin' at the garage wit' Fats and his people. They been askin' bout ya'."

"They don't kno' I'm in town?"

"I ain't tell them but they might kno'."

"Well, I'm goin' out ta' find them a li'l later," I said, getting up and going to my old room.

I put on some Karl Kani jeans and a Minnesota Vikings XXXL T-shirt and starters cap and went outside down state street to see if I could find Fats and T. I. As I was strolling, I saw a police car coming my way. It pulled up by me, and their window came down.

"Yo, Harris. Whassup, man."

I looked and saw that it was Fred. I grew up with him. He was a year older than me and now a cop.

"Whassup, Fred."

"I heard you're big-time now. What team you play for?" Fred asked me.

"The Vikings," I said, grabbing the beak of my hat.

"That's good ta' hear, man. It's changed around here. Lot of violence 'tween each other. I jus' wanted ta' holla at ya'. I'll see you round. And good luck," Fred said, driving off.

When I made it down to the pool hall, I spotted a few guys coming from out of there. It was three o'clock, and I could see Fats and T. I. as I approached them.

"Who's that thurr? James?" T. I. said.

"Oh shit! Whassup, kinfolk," Fats said, hugging me first.

"I thought ya' forgot 'bout us. What's goin' on," T. I. said, grinning from ear to ear.

"Y'all didn't hear that I signed wit' tha Vikings?"

"I thought it was wit' tha Seahawks," a real short brown-skinned dude said who looked familiar, who was with them.

"I got traded after that draft was over," I said, looking at shorty.

"That's Li'l Darryl. You don't remember him. He was a freshman at Eastside your senior year. And was playin' shortstop. The minors had an eye on him," Fats said.

"Okay, I remember," I said, thinking back to my senior year when we used to go to the Eastside baseball games.

Li'l Darryl was the best player on the team.

We went back in the pool hall and started talking about old times until we caught up with the present time. Fats and T. I. were both high school graduates but were into car racing, bike racing, and hustling.

"Man, let's go down to liquor store," Fats said.

As we left the poolroom and turned the corner, a white Maxima pulled up next to us and honked the horn. When I looked at the driver, it was Michelle.

I walked over to the car, and she said, "Hello, James."

"How ya' doin', Michelle?"

"Not too bad. I jus' got off work. Your son been waitin' to see ya'."

"Yeah," she said, unlocking the passenger side of the door.

I got in and didn't bother to say nothing to my boys because I knew where to catch up with them at.

When we got to Michelle's house, I saw my son Kyle lying on the carpet, looking at the television just the way I used to.

"Kyle. Guess who's here," Michelle said.

When he saw me, he immediately got up and came over to me.

"Whassup, li'l man."

"Hi, Daddy," he said with a grin on his face.

He was already tall for a six-year-old, I noticed as I stared at his features.

"That's you all over again, James," Michelle's sister, Faye, said coming in the room with Rollo's son named Roland, who was Michelle's oldest son.

"Yeah. I kno' that's right."

"And congratulation," Faye said. "You're in the NFL with the real players now."

"Thank you," I said, taking a seat on the sofa.

I played arm wrestling with Kyle and Roland on the coffee table and told them about going to the NFL.

"I want to be a football player, Daddy."

"Yeah. Well, you gotta practice."

"I am. I'm too small to play right now."

"Me too," Roland said.

"I know. You two could play wit' each other."

"You can play wit' us, Daddy?"

"Your daddy got things to do. He'll play wit' chu some other time. Y'all get ready to take a bath before ya' eat," Michelle said.

"Okay, Mom. You eatin' wit' us, Dad?"

When Kyle and Roland left the room, Michelle said, "I can see you got married," looking at my ring.

I looked at the ring and said, "Yeah. I forgot to—"

"You don't have to explain."

"I kno'. I was jus' fit'na say that she's from Philly. Where your man at?"

"I don't have one," she said, going into the kitchen.

After eating some meat loaf and macaroni and cheese, Michelle and I talked in the kitchen while she was doing the dishes. I told her I would send money to her every month after giving her five thousand. She never mentioned anything about child support to me since I was away in school, and that made me have more respect for her. I would do for her and my son from the heart. I left Michelle's house a little after eight and went home to my mother's. When I got there, my mother was in the house with her friend, Shirley.

"James, that's you?"

"Yeah, Mama," I said, going inside.

"Ooooh! You are big and handsome. Those women are goin' to be on ya', boy," Shirley said, sounding tipsy while holding a Budweiser can in her hand.

They were playing gin and drinking beer with the stereo playing Al Green. I sat there and drank a beer with them and talked for a little while. My mother noticed the wedding ring on my finger and gave me a look but didn't say nothing. I knew she would later.

"Ma, can I use ya' car for tonight?"

"Yeah, jus' be back 'fore six in the mornin'."

"Aiight," I said, going up the stairs to shower and change clothes. I knew I could catch up with everybody at the Pink Slip Strip Club.

When I got to the Pink Strip, I knew I was back home. Everybody knew me. I still almost knew all the girls who were stripping. Fats, T.

I., and Li'l Darryl were there. I didn't see my li'l brother as of yet, but I knew he would come before it was over.

I let all the strippers get a chance to give me a lap dance and tipped them all. I couldn't wait to come back with some NFL players and let them spend some money on these strippers.

When I got back home, it was a little after five in the morning. I went straight to bed and woke up at eleven when I heard my brother's voice. He was arguing on the phone. I got up and went to use the bathroom and quickly threw on a pair of jeans and sneakers. When I got downstairs, he was eating an egg-'n'-cheese sandwich.

"Man. You woke me up wit' that whinin'."

"Yeah. It was that bitch, Nina. I fucked her couple of times, and now she thinks I'm her man. She left a note on my windshield yesterday in front of the supermarket, and my girl was driving the car."

"Yeah," I said, laughing. "You got problems fa' sure. Nina ain't goin' for that."

"You down wit' OPP?"

"You kno' me," he said back, smiling.

"Drive ya' big bro' to the Lou."

"For what?"

"I want to do something important for y'all before I leave."

When we got to St. Louis, I went straight to the car dealer and traded my brother's Buick Delta in and got him a white Bronco truck. Then we drove out to Forest Park and looked at some mansions. I had in mind to buy my mother a house out there. I wanted to surprise her.

After leaving Forest Park, I was so hungry, so we went over to Mother Fish and got some fish and chips. When we got back home, I grabbed my bags and told my brother to tell Mom and Grandma that I'd be back. I had to go get things in order in Minnesota.

Chapter 6

Tales of Two Cities

Come what may. Time and the hour run through the roughest day.

—William Shakespeare

I was glad the NFL season was starting. Running back and forth from Minnesota to Maryland was wearing me out. Bonnie wouldn't be home until the end of the second season, which meant I had time to go out and learn how to move around Minnesota.

In St. Paul, there was a strip club called the Lamplighter, and in Minneapolis, there was Déjà Vu. I had ventured off to the two clubs with some of the players from the Vikings team. I preferred Minneapolis over St. Paul. There were more people and much more to do. The Mall of America was just being built, and Prince had a club called the Grand Slam that I went to with a couple of players off the team. All the athletes and high rollers went there from Minnesota.

The season started out rough. We were not ready to contend against the elite teams of the NFL. The Minnesota Vikings was in the central division. Chicago Bears, Detroit Lions, and Tampa Bay Buccaneers made up the central division. Even the games against the worst teams such as the Bears and the Buccaneers were rough. I was on the line of scrimmage against the best of them, which made my first season a learning experience. My teammates tried to make it fun for me when we went on the road to play by taking me to hang out. My favorite towns are New York City, Miami, and Green Bay. I looked forward to having a good time because I felt lonely without my wife in jail and family and friends that I grew up with around. I knew once I adjusted to the league, my social life wouldn't be so bad to deal with. We didn't want to stay in Minneapolis after the season because it was boring and too cold. At least back home I knew people, and there were things to do.

I got back home in the late part of January 1992 and bought a house for my mother in St. Louis. When I took her to it, she was expressionless for a minute.

Then she said, "This mine?"

"Yeah, Ma. Let's go inside," I said.

We went inside and I gave her the grand tour of the house.

When we got back downstairs, she said, "It's beautiful, but I'm not movin' in it."

I knitted my brows together, looked at her, and said, "What's wrong?"

"'Cause I'm from East St. Louis. Born and raised. Ya' grandma brought me there and I like it. All my friends are there. I'm not tryin' to get away from them."

"Well, I guess I'll have to sell and give you the money," I said as we walked back to the black 745i BMW I had.

As we drove back home, I decided to upgrade her house. I tried to already upgrade my grandmother's house, but she refused. She didn't even want me to buy her a new floor model television set. All she wanted me to fix was her old color television, which always needed a color tube.

I stayed in East St. Louis for a couple of weeks and even managed to get back on good terms with Michelle. I spent the night with her and my son the last few days before returning to Minnesota. It was the off-season, but I figured I could still hang out with a few of the players. It was the first week of March when I stepped in Déjà Vu, and I met this stripper who I have never seen before. She was a sight for a blind man to see.

As she walked by me, our eyes met, and she said, "Hello."

"How you doin'?" I said with my million-dollar smile.

She looked back and smiled as she kept walking toward the bar. I got up and went to follow her. I ordered some champagne and told her I would like a lap dance in VIP.

When we got up there, I poured her a glass of champagne.

"Don't you want me to dance for you first?"

"Take it easy," I said, passing her a glass.

"Thank you," she said, taking a sip.

"What's your name?"

"Tara. I've been away for a while. Hey, don't you play football?"

"Yeah."

"I thought I seen you in Grand Slam with some football players."

"Yeah. My name is James."

"You come here a lot?"

"Yeah. You were gone a long time."

"I had a baby."

"Anyone I know?"

"I doubt it. He left and went back to Chicago. Fuck him. I can take care of mines by myself."

"It's like that, huh?"

"It's like that," she said, finishing off her drink.

I poured some more in her glass and mine, and she said, "I'm still working and don't want to be on bread too long."

"What is that s'ppose to mean? I'm a customer."

"Well, let me treat you like one," she said, getting up and going into her dancing routine.

I watched her petite body move to the rhythm of Snoop and Dr. Dre's "Nuthin' But a G Thang."

After the song went off, I gave her a fifty-dollar bill and said, "You do your job very well."

"I try to satisfy all my customers."

"Well, I'm not satisfied," I said, grabbing her by her G-string and pulling her close to me.

"Stop! What're you doing?" Tara said with a smile on her face.

"I told ya', I'm not satisfied."

"I don't fool around wit' my customers," she said, pushing my hands away.

"I'm not tryin' to fool wit' chu. I want your digits."

Tara gave me her phone number after a little more conversation, and I continued having fun for the rest of the night when a few of the football and basketball players came inside. Of course, Tara was watching my every move. That's when I knew I had to have her. She had a baby but didn't have any stretch marks showing from it.

The following weekend, Tara and I left Déjà Vu and went to her apartment on Lindell. I spent the night with her while her mother kept her daughter, whose name was Tiara. Tara was originally from California. Her mother moved here when she was a little girl, so Tara could have a better life. Whatever that was supposed to mean because Tara was stuck to raise a daughter on her own as a stripper.

We got to know each other a little better and had a few things in common.

Since my father lived in LA, I used to visit him in Compton every summer when I was growing up. Tara's aunt still lived in Inglewood, so we talked about California. She even told me that she used to talk to a Crip for LA in Minneapolis altogether. Tara and I were hanging out all the time now.

On the weekend of Easter, Tara and I went to the Grand Slam together. Word was out that Prince was going to be there. When we got in the club, it was jam-packed. Tara and I got separated for a little while because I ran into people I knew, and she did too. When we got back up with each other, it was by the bar. This dark-skinned medium-built roughneck-looking dude was buying her a drink. She spotted me and immediately called me over.

When I got over by her, she said, "James, I want you to meet Patch."

I nodded my head and said, "What up."

"Whassup. Ain't you playin' fa' the Vikings?"

"Yeah."

"I thought so. I've seen ya' 'round town. And I see ya' finally found good people to be around Tara. What they call ya'?"

"Harris."

"What ya' drinkin'?"

"Jack Daniels."

"Whew! That's some hard shit," Patch said, calling for the bartender.

After he ordered some drinks, we sat at a table and talked for a while. I found out he was from LA and was down in Minnesota hustling. Even though he wasn't polished, I was getting good vibes from being around him. He was straight up, that much I could tell. He and Tara were tight, but it didn't look like they were having a sexual relationship.

When he left the table to go talk to a couple of dudes, Tara said, "I used to talk to his friend but nothing happened between us. He went back to LA."

"Why you tellin' me that?"

"'Cause…I don't want you thinking the wrong thing about me. He's not my type."

I looked at her and smiled. I knew she wasn't lying. Patch had a patch over his left eye. He wasn't naturally ugly, but he was a little too hard on the eyes for any female that's into looks.

He came back over to the table and said, "Pardon me. I had to holla at them 'bout somethin' important."

I could tell what that important meant and said, "I understand."

After drinking my drink, Patch and I both looked at Tara. I could tell he wanted to hang out with me, so I gave him my cell phone number. We enjoyed the performance by Morris Day and Prince and had no time for anybody else. We went to Tara's apartment.

*****

It was Sunday noon when my cell phone rang at home.

I picked it up and heard a voice say, "What up, Harris."

"Whassup, Patch."

"You ate yet?"

"Nah. I just got up when you rang."

"Why don't you meet me at TGIF?"

"Aiight. I'll be there in a half hour," I said, hanging up and going to the bathroom.

When I pulled up to park the Range Rover, I could see Patch's white 300 Benz in the handicap parking space. I guess he considered himself legally blind. I went inside the restaurant and spotted him at the table in the corner of the restaurant.

"I already ordered some food," Patch said while holding his hand out to me.

I shook it and said, "You couldn't wait for me?" with a smile on my face.

"Man…'cuz I was starvin'."

I called the waiter over to the table and ordered a T-bone steak, french fries, and shrimps.

After the waiter left, Patch said, "I'm glad Tara introduced me to you. She's good people."

"Yeah, she is."

"When I came to Minny, my man was pushing up on her, and she used to let us stay at her crib."

"Yeah. She didn't tell me that."

"Yeah. Anyway, cuz shot a kid down the block from her crib on 25th and Lindell last summer and never came back," Patch said as the waiter brought his food.

"I'll be back wit' yours in about five minutes," the young White boy said, walking away.

"That left me wit' a lot of drama to deal wit' because I wasn't leaving. It's sweet out here and Mt. Airy in St. Paul. You can ask around 'bout me. There are stories to go wit' this face. Some are true and some are false."

"I'm 'bout getting money as smooth as possible. I avoid the drama," I said.

As the dude came back with my food, we got silent until he left. Then we started talking about basketball.

"My man is from Oakland. He's goin' to bring heat to Minnesota. He's good people."

"Yeah," I said cutting into my steak. "Yo, cuz, I want to show you somethin' after we done eatin'."

We finished eating and left a twenty-dollar tip. Patch paid for both our meals. Then I drove to Tara's apartment and parked the

Range in front of there and rode with Patch out to St. Paul. He took me to Laurel Street and parked in front of a house. We got out and walked down the block until we came to an off-white painted house. He knocked on the door, and a frail-backed woman opened the door.

"What ya' doin' openin' tha door?" Patch said.

"'Cause they all in tha kitchen," the frail woman said.

I followed Patch to the kitchen and couldn't believe what I saw. Two bricks of cocaine were on the table with paraphernalia and crackheads were by the stove. Two were cooking and one was smoking a pipe.

"Yo, Mel, what the fuck you got all these muthafuckas in here for?" Patch screamed.

"Ma…man, I…I…I…I needed them to…to…to test the shit," Mel stammered.

"You don't need all these muthafuckas. You two, let's go," Patch said, grabbing a dude by the stove smoking and a White girl who was sitting at the table in a daze.

"Get off me," the White girl said.

"Bitch! Who the fuck ya' talkin' to," Patch said smacking her to the floor. "Get to steppin', you funky bitch."

"Audrey!" she yelled. "This ain't ya' house," the White girl said.

The frail Black woman came into the kitchen and looked at the scene.

"Tell him who I am," the White girl said.

"I already kno' who you are. A crackhead bitch!" Patch said, kicking her in the ass…

The White girl screamed out in pain, got up off the floor, and high stepped out the door. I knew I shouldn't have left my car behind. I was ready to go. What if she went and told the police?

Patch was in full boss player mode after that. He was instructing everybody what to do. He told the frail Black woman to get everybody out of the kitchen too. I had to listen to Patch bark instructions at Mel. Mel listened and nodded his head like a little boy would do whatever.

When Patch finished, he turned toward me and said, "Ya' ready, cuz?"

I wanted to say, "I shouldn't never come wit'chu." But I said, "Let's ride."

As we drove back to Minneapolis, he let me know that was his other operation in St. Paul and Mel was from there. He met him in the Lamplighter and clicked right off with him because Mel looked up to him. Then Patch told me about the shoot-outs he had in Minnesota and how he got shot with a shotgun and the pellets messed his left eye up. He had a missing lung form getting shot in Cali already too, but he was a soldier. He shot up St. Paul and Minneapolis locals and ran some Chicago boys out of the state. Now he was the man. His original name is Patrick, but now that he had one eye and wore a path over the bad one, everybody called him Patch.

I let Patch know that I could get him as many bricks as he needed and get it safely into Minnesota without any problems.

"What do you want from me?" Patch said as we pulled up in front of Tara's apartment.

"All I want is for you to play it fair with me. We can split the money down the middle."

"You got that, cuz. My word is all I got, but it means a lot," Patch said, holding his hand out.

I shook it, and that sealed our relationship.

Chapter 7

The Double Life

Play to the people's fantasies.

—Robert Greene

As spring came, the trees and flowers started blossoming and so did the drug money. I gave Patch ten birds to work with, and he moved them with no problem in a little over a week. I didn't know that Minnesota had that many cocaine users, so I got twenty-five birds for Patch the next time. My Mexican connection in Philly introduced me to a few Mexicans down in Houston, Texas, and I was now going there to pick up my work.

By the end of April, Patch was driving in Alabaster with a 745i BMW that I helped him get by trading in his 300 E Mercedes Benz and adding a little more cash. The next thing I did was get Tara a new apartment and used the old one as a stash house for the drug money. I then decided to take a vacation with a few of the players who had a restaurant business in Puerto Rico. I gave Tara the keys to the condo and told her to take care of the spot while I was gone away on business.

It was four of us going to Puerto Rico. The two going on business were Jeff and Ron. Fred and I was just going for pleasure.

It was the month of May, and the weather was nice and warm when we got off the plane in San Juan International. We went straight over to the Thrifty Car Rental, where there was two Lincoln Continentals waiting for us. I rode with Ron because he invited me. We all had reservations at the Wyndham El San Juan Hotel and Casino for free because Jeff and Ron were known as high rollers in the casino. While I was unpacking, I took my Ray-Ban reversible mirror glasses out and decided to wear them the whole time while in Puerto Rico. I had just finished unpacking when Ron came in the room.

"Hey, Harris, me, and Jeff is going to check out the seafood restaurant while Fred takes a nap. You wanna come or what?"

"Yeah. I want to see y'all restaurant." I threw on a Karl Kani pair of jeans and shirt and left out of the room with my Ray-Ban glasses on.

Jeff drove the car with Ron sitting in the front and me in the back.

"This is going to be the new tourist spot," Jeff said. "That's why I told Ron about it last year, so we can beat the rush."

"Yeah, I see they got a Hard Rock Café."

"That's nothing. Wait until you go to party. The women down here are hot, young, and fine," Ron said, shaking his head.

When we got to Santiago's Restaurant, it was half full, but it was five thirty. It had a Caribbean atmosphere. The manager took us in the back, and it had a wine cellar stocked with assortments of fine wines. There were rooms for dining or social events and a bar. I could see they made a wise investment. I ordered fried oysters with confetti rice and she-crab soup. I didn't want to start drinking yet, so I drank a pear nectar juice. The food was good. I could see that Santiago's Seafood Restaurant had food and good service. My meal alone was priced at twenty dollars and some change.

After I finished eating, Jeff was the first to say, "How did you like the food?"

"It was on point," I said.

"Good. Because the chef is my brother-in-law."

"Oh, yeah?" I said.

"Yeah," Ron said, walking up. "It's a family thing. I just wanted to get involved too."

"True dat. You see the potential," Jeff said, smiling and winking his eye.

We went back to the car and drove back to the hotel. Fred wasn't in his room. We knew he was in the casino. I was the first to go downstairs and catch him at the blackjack table. All of us knew this was his obsession. When I got there, he was up two grand. I could see through my Ray-Ban glasses two fine women in floral dresses and sandals staring at me and smiling. The rearview glasses were working fine as I watched them staring at me. As soon as I turned toward their direction, they switched their glances to somebody else and were giggling. I knew they were young and full of games. I could play games very well too. I pulled out a bankroll and bought some chips and started playing blackjack. I now had their attention.

By the time Jeff and Ron came downstairs, I was up two thousand, and Fred was up five thousand. The table started getting filled with gamblers, and a crowd was around us, including the two girls. I just used my rearview glasses to watch them. Jeff and Ron got in the game, and everybody started losing. I stopped while I was ahead six hundred dollars. Fred lost everything he had won and was down three thousand.

We all went up to our rooms and changed to go clubbing. Jeff said he'd met his wife in this club called Rio Grande. I put on my crème-colored tailored silk shirt and pants with matching gators. I only wore my diamond stud earrings and a Philippe Patek timepiece. Jeff and Ron had their tailored best on too.

When we walked in the club, the salsa sounded good, and to my surprise, I saw the two women who were at the casino by the bar. They had on shorter dresses with heels now. Jeff was talking to a middle-aged Hispanic man, and Ron and Fred were over by the bar, so I decided to go over to talk to the ladies. I know my *Española* was no *bien*, but I had to say something to them.

I approached them and said, "What are you ladies drinking?" and pointed at the bar.

"I speak English," the olive-skinned one said.

"Oh, yeah? Good because I don't speak Spanish," I said, smiling.

"We both like tequila."

"Good. Woman of my taste."

The other girl said something in Spanish, and they both started laughing. I walked off to the bar, wondering what she said.

By the time I retuned with the girls' drinks, Fred was on my heels. "I see you made some friends."

I turned to the ladies and said, "My name is James, and this is my amigo, Fred."

"My friend's name is Alicia, and my name is Judy," the olive-skinned girl said.

She had the most desirable shape. Her waist was small, and her hips were wide. The dress she wore was clinging to her body like a nightgown. Her friend Alicia had a cinnamon complexion and big breasts. Judy was by far the prettiest.

"What are you doing here?" Judy asked me over the salsa music that was playing.

Alicia was moving in place to the beat as Fred went to her side.

"I came with some friends who are down here on some business."

"I see. You come to sightsee."

"You could say that because I see a sight I like already," I said, making her smile and seeing her teeth that were perfectly straight and white.

Fred and Alicia went to the dance floor after finishing their drinks while Judy drank hers and ate the worm along with me. Then I ordered two more tequilas. She drank the second one down in one motion, so I did the same thing. I wasn't about to let her outdo me.

"I see you like tequilas."

"Yeah. They all right," Judy said in English but with a Spanish flavor. "You want to drink some Don?"

"Yeah," I said, getting up and ordering a fifth.

When I got back to the table, we drank the whole bottle while talking. I was surprised how she held her liquor. I told her I was a football player, and she told me she was a stewardess ready to attend college. She wanted to be a pediatrician. She still lived with her parents in Caparra Heights in Puerto Rico. Fred and Alicia came and sat back down, so we decided to go dance. I let her lead while I followed.

"I see you can learn to do the salsa steps," Judy said, moving to the beat easily with her hips.

"I'm a quick learner," I said, moving with her. To me, it was like doing the step and having dry sex.

I was feeling good of the run, or was it the tequila, when we stopped. I was sweating like a politician as we made it back to the table.

I gave Judy my card with my cell phone number on it and said, "Here you go. You can all me anytime you want."

"Anytime?"

"That's what I said," I said, smiling at her.

Fred and Alicia came back to the table, and Fred wasn't looking to happy. He talked to me and Judy the rest of the time at the table. That's when I told Judy I was down here for a week and that we could hang out some more. She agreed, and Fred and I left the lady's side.

On the way back to the hotel, Fred told me that he couldn't talk to Alicia because she couldn't speak English.

The following day, I went out and left the crew in the casino. I knew Jeff and Ron had business to take care of at the restaurant, so Judy came and picked me up, after she called me, an hour later in the casino in a Pontiac Bonneville. We went to the ferry first. She showed me everything she possibly could and then we got back at the hotel at four thirty. We went and ate at a tropical bar and grill and promised to see each other the following day.

It was eight in the morning when the crew came to my room.

"Come play golf with us. It'll only be a few hours," Jeff said when I opened the door.

"Aiight. Let me take a shower to wake up," I said, going into the bathroom.

I knew I told Judy to meet me in the casino at one, but I had some time to kill. This was my third time playing golf, so I shot a handicap of ninety-one. Jeff had the best game and shot a seventy-two while Fred and Ron were in the eighties.

It was going on three o' clock when we got back to the hotel. I didn't hear from Judy the whole day as I decided to go with the crew to the beach named Isle Verde. I had my Ray-Ban glasses on and couldn't stop looking at the women that were on the beach. They all looked young. Judy had told me she was twenty-one. Her birthday just passed in March.

"My birthday is tomorrow, and I would be twenty-six," I had told Judy that and was expecting to see her.

We left the beach, went back to the hotel, and gambled all night. The phone woke me up the next day.

I picked up the phone and said, "Yeah."

"Is that the way you speak to your Reina on your birthday."

"Whassup, girl. I see you remembered."

"Of course. That's why I called you early before you went out."

I looked at the clock and it was 9:00 a.m.

"I want to take you somewhere. You are my Negro, Rey, okay?"

"You're what?"

"Black king. I'm coming over there," she said, hanging up the phone on me.

Before Judy came, I called my crew and told them don't come by the room because I got company. I was in the shower when Judy came, but I left the door open for her to come in and wait. I came out the bathroom with just a towel around my waist.

"Hmm…I didn't know you looked like that without no shirt on," she said, smiling and not taking her eyes off my body.

"You want to see me in my birthday suit?"

"Yeah, put it on," she said.

I started loosening the towel around my waist, and she said, "What're you doing?"

"Showing you my birthday suit."

I walked over toward Judy and grabbed her shoulders. Then I started kissing her. Her hands went straight between her legs.

When I pushed her on the bed, she said, "No, James."

I looked down at her and she explained to me that she was a virgin and wasn't planning on having sex until she got married; I respected what she said and got off her.

She took me to meet her family. Their last name was Krude. Her mother couldn't speak English, but her father was a doctor while her mother took care of the home. Her brother had a dog and a parrot for pets. He was fifteen years old and seemed to be spoiled.

Afterward, we went out to eat at Chills Grill and Bar and ate baby back ribs. Then we went to Mayaguez Mall, and she bought a summer Guess outfit.

When we got back to the hotel room, Judy said, "Do you mind if I change my clothes over here?"

"Nah. Go ahead," I said.

"Can I take a shower first?"

"Make yourself at home."

Judy went to go take a shower, and I turned on the radio and started searching the stations when I heard her say, "James!"

I went to the door and said, "Whassup?"

"Come in here. I won't bite you."

I went inside, and she said, "You wanna take a shower with me?"

I couldn't believe what I was hearing. Was she playing games?

"Hold on," I said nonchalantly.

When I got in the shower, she had soap on her body. I scrubbed her back. She had soft skin. I kept scrubbing her back then my erection brushed against her ass cheek. I started kissing her neck and stroking her clit with my right middle finger.

"*Te gustaria probaia?*"

"You wanna try it?"

I didn't even answer her; I just tried to put it in from behind. She grabbed my dick and put it in her anal cavity slowly with the help of the soap and water.

I couldn't believe it when I had it halfway inside her, and she said, "*Rompem el culo carino!*"

I didn't understand what she said, but I knew she liked what I was doing to her. I started pumping in and out of her slowly while using my right hand to play with her private area. Her black silky hair came down her back, so I ran my finger through it too.

She was moaning, and if after a few minutes, she said, "Ooh! *No puedo creer lo*. I'm cumming."

I came along with her and let the water from the shower run down between our bodies. We stayed in the shower and went another round just having oral sex.

*****

The rest of the trip, I was with my boys and didn't see Judy. She had my number and knew where I was at, so I wasn't going to sweat her.

When we were getting on the plane to go back to Minnesota, to my surprise, I saw Judy. She was working on my flight. I pointed her out to my crew and took my seat in first class.

It was no surprise when she came over to me and said, "Hola. Are you comfortable?"

She reached over my head and removed a pillow which I knew was there. When she put it behind my head, I turned my neck and smelled her perfume scent. I took a chance and nuzzled my nose in her neck, not caring who came up and down the aisle.

"I couldn't help it. You smell good."

"Why didn't you answer my message?"

"What message?" I said, knitting my brows.

"The one I left for you yesterday morning."

"I didn't go by the desk yesterday or check the phone service. Just call me when I get home."

"I will, *mi rey*," Judy said, sashaying away.

When I got back home, everything looked all right until I went to put my timepiece back in the case; I noticed the other there were missing. I called Tara and asked her if she knew anything about it. Of course, she said no. But she let me know she brought two people over there. Kia and her man, Brian, a.k.a. Busy Bee. I knew Patch didn't like him because he was a petty hustler who wanted to see Patch fall off.

When I got to the stash apartment, Patch was there counting money with the money machine.

"Whassup, Harris."

"Ain't shit."

"Had a ball out there in PR, huh?"

"Yeah. I met a dime piece. She's a piece of work."

"That's good. I kno' you bust her down."

"Oh yeah. Fa' sure… Hey, you kno' Kia, right?"

"What about her?"

"Tara had her over my house, and I think she took my watch collection."

"What! I kno' where the trifling bitch stay. Let me finish counting this loot, we'll pay her a visit," Patch said, grabbing a 9 mm from under the sofa cushion.

I got in my ride and followed Patch. I wasn't about to ride with him. I knew he had a gun on him too.

We drove over to the Plymouth section, and it was about seven thirty. Patch rang the bell and wet got buzzed in. We went up to her apartment and rang the bell. She opened the door, and Patch kicked her back into the living room and onto the floor.

He pulled out his gun and said, "Bitch! Where tha fuck iz my man'z watches?"

"I didn't have nothin' to do wit' it. I swear. Brian took them."

"You let him do it," Patch said, ripping her shirt off as he picked her up and threw her on the leather sofa.

I closed the door and looked at Patch go into his madman role.

"I should make you suck both our dicks at the same time," he said, squeezing one of her breasts. "But I don't have time to play games wit' ya'." He held the gun between her legs and said, "Where are the watches?"

"Let me go get them," Kia said with tears coming down her cheeks.

Patch let her get up and followed her to the bedroom. I waited in the living room.

She brought out two of them, and I said, "There is still one missing."

"I promise I will get it for you."

"You better or there will be some serious repercussions," Patch said, smacking her so hard that snot came from out her nose.

When I got home that night, I called Tara and told her everything. She swore she didn't know. She told me that I could come over her house because she couldn't leave her daughter alone. I hung up the phone, and it immediately started ringing again.

I picked it up thinking it was Tara and heard a Spanish accent and knew it was Judy. She told me she was ready to come see me because she missed me. I told her to take a flight to Minnesota, and I'll pick her up at the airport. That night, I sat up and thought out a master plan. I would set up a fake wedding. I called East St. Louis and was talking to Fats. I explained to him that I wanted to set up a fake wedding. He told me he would be out there tomorrow with T. I. and Li'l Darryl.

They beat Judy to Minnesota, and I explained everything I wanted to do to them. We decided on a plan after about fifteen minutes. I went and bought Li'l Darryl a reverend outfit from a costume shop out of the mall and a two-carat ring and some wedding bands. I went and got Judy from the airport while the boys stayed back and prepared everything. Judy was all smiles when she saw me.

"Hola, James. I took a three-day sick leave, so I got five days to be with you."

"That's good because I got a surprise for you," I said, opening the case and showing her the ring.

She was surprised. She hugged me and said, "So we're engaged now, but I can't do nothing with you until we're married."

I looked at her with a wry smile and said, "I want to marry you as soon as we get home. I got some friends and a reverend waiting for us," showing her the wedding bands.

"But I...I don't have nothing to wear."

"Yes, you do. Pick it out at the bridal shop. We're going there right now," I said, grabbing her hand.

We got there and she picked out a white gown that represented virginity. I picked out a tuxedo, and we got home a little after four.

Li'l Darryl didn't have time to memorize the wedding script we got for him off the internet, so he hid it inside the Bible and said it verbatim after we walked down the stairs of the condo to the living room. Prince's "Dove Cry" was playing.

When I slipped the ring on her finger, I could see that Judy really believed this fantasy. Tears of joy came from her eyes. Judy probably thought we were laughing out of happiness, but we were laughing at Li'l Darryl acting like a reverend. Fats and T. I. were in tears as I called a few players to come by the condo with their wives and girls for a little reception party. To my surprise, Jeff and his wife Lynda came by. Lynda knew Judy's father in Puerto Rico because she used to go to the hospital he worked at. Judy now had a friend she could talk to when she moved to Minnesota to be with me.

Chapter 8

A Tangled Web Weaved

Plan all the way to the end.

—Robert Greene

Judy and I stayed in the house for three days making love. The last night, we made love for four hours straight. We were good sex partners. She had no inhibitions, and to top it all off, she had a lot of confidence in herself.

Before going back home, she told me that she'd be back to move in by the end of June. She had to transfer her stewardess job to Minnesota. I decided to call Tara as soon as Judy left. I didn't talk to her in a while, so I told her I was at football camp. She told me to come by her house because she had something to tell me that she didn't want to talk about over the phone.

When I got there, I was expecting her to say something about me being with another woman, but instead she told me that Patch had shot at Kia's man at the club called Jerseys. He'd missed him but hit some innocent bystanders. It was war between them now.

"You don't need to be around him, James."

"That's my man. You should'na brought nobody wit'chu to my house and all of this wouldn't be happenin'," I said, a little upset because Tara was telling me who I should be around.

I left Tara's apartment and went to find Patch. When I couldn't find him, I called an emergency number he'd given me, but there was no answer there either. I decided to let him contact me since I had to go to minicamp and visit Bonnie.

It wasn't until after the Fourth of July that I caught up with Patch at the stash house. He was counting some money when he came in.

"What up, cuz."

"Long time no see," I said, locking the door.

"Yeah, I kno'. I had to shake the town for a while right. I kno' ya' heard. That bitch called popo on me tryin' to protect that bitch ass Busy Bee."

"Don't worry about it. Leave it alone," I said.

I didn't want us to stop getting money over a watch. I eventually convinced Patch to leave it alone and started talking business with him. He told me everything was going smoothly, and he had put some money in his safe for me. I got it out, and the following day, I made the trip to Texas and brought him back more bricks.

Everything was running smoothly by the end of the July when Judy came to live with me. Every day for the first two weeks, we made love.

Then I had to get ready play preseason. This was my excuse to come home late because she was starting to be too clingy.

The week after preseason, I went to visit Bonnie. I explained to Judy that I had to go to minicamp and couldn't stay in town.

When I got Maryland, I spent the whole weekend with Bonnie doing quickies. I told her the season was going to start, and I wouldn't be able to come visit her anymore. She cried but understood.

When I got back to Minnesota, it was Monday. I had a game that coming Sunday. Judy wasn't going to be home until night at 11:00 p.m. to 6:00 a.m., and her only day off was Sunday, which was the hardest day in my profession. At least now she couldn't smother me with her love and affection. We got along very well in bed. That part of the relationship was just fine.

When I went away on road games, I had to hire a cleanup service because Judy didn't have time to do household chores or cook for that matter.

My second season in the league was a lot easier because I was familiar with the players I played against. Athletic ability isn't all you need to play football. You could lack speed or strength and make it up with fundamentals, intelligence of the game, and knowing who you're up against. For instance, Green Bay is always a scrimmage because he was stiff-arming me and holding me. When I told him to stop doing it and he didn't, I put a move on him that I picked up from our defensive line coach, Big John, which snapped a bone in his elbow.

As the season ended, we had a good enough record to make the playoffs. We lost to the Washington Redskins 24-7, and the season was over. I came home, and Judy had taken a vacation from her job. This was the first time we were around each other for more than a day since our marriage. We made love, and she woke me up the next morning with breakfast on a tray.

"*Buenos manana, mi rey*," she said, placing the tray in front of me. I sat up in the bed and she said, "You want me to feed you?"

"That would be nice," I said.

There were scrambled eggs, blueberry waffles, and sausage links on the plate. She cut the waffles up for me and started feeding me. I felt like a king for real.

"You like?"

"Mm hmm. I like," I said, chewing the food.

"What do you think about having a party?" Judy said, pausing with the food on the fork to hear my answer.

"Where at? In here."

"Yeah. We don't never do nothing together," she said in her Spanglish accent.

I knew that whenever she talked like that, it meant she wanted something from me real bad.

"Who do you plan on inviting?"

"Just a couple of friends I work with and Lynda."

"We can do that. I'm down," I said, opening my mouth for more food.

Judy loosened the silk robe she had on and leaned over to give me some food. She was wearing nothing under the robe. She knew how to tease me because I felt myself getting aroused at the sight of her body.

The weekend came quickly. I invited T. I. and Fats down from East Boogie. They said Li'l Darryl was upset he couldn't come because he had pretended to be the minister that married us. Jeff and Lynda came along and brought another couple with them. In front of my condo looked like a car show with Beemers, Benzes, and Range Rovers parked and shining. Patch came through wearing a Baldessarini ensemble and was eyeing Judy's coworkers and friends, who were Leandra and Richelle. Leandra was all sister with an attitude and confidence. Some people call her stuck-up. Richelle was biracial and more of an introvert. She had the prettiest hazel eyes to go with her smile. I invited over a few more of the fellas from the team to make it more fun. Leandra and Richelle were getting all the attention from the guys. I kept a nice CD collection so that the music never stopped playing.

By midnight, everybody was having a good time. The cognac, beer, and vodka were the most popular drinks. Patch, T. I., and Leandra were the only ones drinking the champagne. Patch was getting too aggressive with Leandra. He had her by the arm, dragging her to the dance floor when he heard me playing Naughty by Nature's, "OPP."

One of the players went over to the dance with them, and Patch shoved him away from Leandra and said, "Get the tha fuck away from her."

I could tell what was going to happen next, so I made my way into the area they were at and said, "You'll aiight?"

"Yeah. We're aiight," Patch said, grabbing Leandra and himself in the closet.

She was banging on the door to get out. I tried to ignore the incident by going into the kitchen where Judy, Jeff, and Lynda were, but Richelle came complaining to me, so I went and got them out there. He came out laughing. The incident changed the atmosphere of the party because all the football players left a little while after. Then Judy's girlfriends left with Patch following behind Leandra.

Fats and T. I. were spending the night. It was 3:00 a.m. when Jeff and Lynda left, and Judy went to bed

Fats and T. I. looked at me.

"What ya' gonna do when Bonnie come home?" Fats said.

"Man...I don't kno', kinfolk. I'ma figure something out. I can't have her here too much longer."

"That was some nickel slick shit you did to her, but it's gonna be worth it," T. I. said laughing.

"Hell yeah!" I said smiling. "She's one of a kind in the bedroom."

"I could imagine. She's fine as hell," Fats said.

"Man, you jus' don't kno'. I gotta go," I said, leaving them sitting in the living room, hooking up the PlayStation.

*****

I woke up in the morning, and Judy was getting dressed.

"Where are you going?"

"Nowhere. I just don't want to be naked with your friends in the house."

"They know not to come in here."

"Better safe than sorry. Did you see how your friend Patch was acting? I don't like him."

"Who are you to talk about him and choosing who I should be around?" I said in a defensive tone.

I figured this was the time to make her think she was on my bad side. I only had a few months before Bonnie came home. On top of it all, she was pregnant.

"I didn't say who you should be around. I'm just concerned because I'm your woman."

"Not telling me who to be around, you ain't. My mother is in East St. Louis," I said, getting out of the bed and going to the bathroom.

When I came out, Judy had gone downstairs. When I got down there, she had cooked breakfast for everybody. But that wasn't stopping my plan. I left out the condo and didn't come back for two days. I stayed at the apartment with Fats and T. I. I took them to the

Rolex and Déjà Vu clubs. They fucked a few of the strippers at a hotel before going back home.

When I came back home, Judy was not there but left a note that read, "I'll be home early, *mi rey*. Love Judy."

I left out and went to stay with Tara. I was going to avoid Judy as if she had the plague.

When Valentine's Day came and I didn't show up at home, she couldn't take it any longer and went through all my property until she found Tara's number.

When she called, I picked up the phone, and she said, "*Se acabo el juego*."

"What?" I said.

"I found your bitch number. I hope she has some good *cono* because I'm gonna fuck her up when I see her."

"You trippin'."

"No! You trippin'. You better be here tonight or else I'm coming to that bitch's house tonight."

"Do what'cha gotta do," I said, hanging up the phone.

Tara asked me who it was, and I told her it was a girl I went out with that found her number and called it. I never let Tara in on the fake wedding. She can't hold water and would tell somebody that may know somebody that knows Judy.

To my surprise, Judy didn't come by. I went home the next morning, and she wasn't there. I decided to stay away and let her cool down. I didn't particularly feel safe sleeping around her.

The following week, I stayed home and waited for Saturday night. It was now March and I had to get her out of the apartment and get rid of her things too. When she got home, she saw me in the living room looking at the television and walked right by me without even saying nothing. I got up from the sofa and went to find her. She was sitting in the jacuzzi when I walked into the bathroom.

"We need to have a serious talk."

"That's why I'm here," I said, clearing my throat.

"I think we need to spend some time apart. We might've rushed into this marriage thing."

"What! *No puedo creer lo!* You giving up this easy on us. I guess it's my fault."

"I didn't say it was your fault. Listen… I'm going to get another apartment and you can stay there for a while."

"Oh, so now you throwing me out. I hate you!" Judy said, throwing a bar of soap at me.

I ducked and heard it hit the wall. I started to go choke her but knew that's what she wanted me to do, so I left out the bathroom. Judy came in the bedroom, got in the bed with me, and didn't say a word. I kept my back toward her, and she reached her hand over my body to feel my manhood. She started caressing it and then pulling it.

"*Mi cachonda. Te quiero mucho,*" she said.

I gave in to her requests and my wants. I made love to her every way I possibly could. I was going to miss having this woman at my side.

It was on the last Monday of April when Bonnie came home. I had been preparing for her arrival cleaning up the condo. She didn't want no party because she didn't know anybody in Minnesota and was also seven months pregnant. I didn't tell Tara about her, nor did Judy know about Bonnie. I got Judy a nice apartment near downtown Minneapolis. This way, she wasn't too far away from anything.

When Bonnie arrived, it was almost three o'clock. I saw her getting off the plane and walked over to her, and she grabbed me around my waist.

"I missed you, James."

"I missed you too. Come on. Let's go home," I said.

I put her luggage in the back seat of the Range, and we got in the front.

I rubbed her stomach, and she said, "What's that for?"

"I missed him too."

"How do you know it's a he?"

"Trust me. That's what it is," I said, pulling off.

When we got home, Bonnie walked inside the condo and said, "This is nice but—"

"But what?" I said, putting the luggage down and closing the door.

"It needs a woman's touch."

"Well, Mrs. Harris, that's where you come in," I said, putting my hand around her waist and giving her a sloppy kiss.

"James...ooh, stop!" Bonnie shouted as I ran my hands across her body. "Let's wait till later."

"Aiight. I got food already cooked for us."

"You do?"

"Of course, girl."

"I love you with all my heart."

"I know," I said, kissing her again and pulling loose the drawstrings to her pants.

"James."

"What?" I said while kissing her neck.

"Can I see the house first?"

"Aiight, but it's on afterwards."

I showed her the four bedrooms, dining room, living room, two bathrooms, the kitchen, and two guest rooms. Then I went to get the food ready for us to eat dinner.

While Bonnie sat in the jacuzzi, I put out broiled shrimp with fried rice and salmon on the table. I had cran-apple ocean spray for her and the baby and some Jack Daniels for me.

While we were eating, we talked about what I was doing while she was locked up and then about taking a much-deserved vacation together.

When Bonnie saw me pouring my third glass of JD, she said, "What are you planning on doing to me?"

"What ya' mean by that?" I said, smiling.

"You entirely too full to be running up in me."

"No, I'm not," I said, getting up and going over to her.

I picked her up, and she said, "What are you doing?"

"It's about that time."

"Don't drop me," she said as I took her upstairs to our king-size bed.

I laid Bonnie down, removed her straps, and kissed her on the neck. I worked my way down to her breasts. They were swollen from the pregnancy. By the time I worked my tongue down between Bonnie's legs, she was breathing hard. I worked my tongue until it started getting tired. By then I could tell she had climaxed because she was sprawled out on the bed in a five-point position. I climbed back up to look at her face and kissed her gently before entering her. I went in slowly. She was wet but tight. I was scared to put my weight on her, so I held myself up off her and stroked slowly.

"Ooh…James. I love you. I want you to come in me," Bonnie said, spreading her legs wider.

I picked up a little momentum and drove deep inside of her, and she jumped.

"What's wrong?" I said, stopping.

"Nothing, why'd you stop?"

"Why'd you jump?"

"It hurt a little but don't stop."

I pulled out of her and said, "Turn on your side."

Bonnie got on her side, and I lifted her leg up and slid back inside of her. This time, I put it in all the way, and she moaned. I knew I couldn't hurt her in this position, so I worked her until I felt her trembling. I then turned her over to her hands and knees. The JD had me numb. I worked Bonnie doggy style but was careful not to hurt her. When I finally was about to cum, Bonnie threw it back at me.

"Hmm, James. You wanted me bad."

"Hmm, mmm" was all I said.

We talked a little while until Bonnie went and used the bathroom.

When she came back into the bedroom, I said, "Come here."

She looked between my legs and said, "Damn! You didn't have enough?"

"I've been waiting a long time for this day."

"I can tell," she said, getting back in bed with me.

The next day, the phone woke us up. Bonnie answered it and said, "It's for you," and dropped the phone on my chest.

"Hello."
"James. Who was that answering the phone?"
"My wife."
"What!"
"She just got here yesterday."
"You never told me you were married," Tara said, surprised.
"You never asked. I'll talk to ya' later," I said, hanging up.
"Who was that?" Bonnie said with an attitude.
"Jus' a friend."
"Yeah right. I know you, James. You fucked her. I'm not gonna be out here fighting with these bitches over you."
"You just got her and trippin'."
"No. You're trippin'. Remember, we're married."
"I know. That's why you shouldn't be trippin'," I said, getting out of bed and going to the bathroom.

That was only the beginning of what was to come. We would have many more arguments between us. I explained that whole situation to Tara and she understood. She didn't care anyhow or anyway. As long as I was taking care of her bills, she was happy.

The following weeks, Bonnie decorated the house and bought new furniture and a new bed. She gave the house a Mediterranean look. She bought a Swedish posturepedic sofa that I fell in love with. I slept on it a few times coming in late at night and hearing Bonnie's mouth. The baby's room was in canary yellow with every possible baby toy you could think of. The crib was almost big enough for me to sleep in.

Patch turned out to be trustworthy and reliable. I had gotten ten birds for him, and he was handling business. It was now May, and he talked about business picking up when summer came.

When June came, I had to go to minicamp, so I made sure I collected some money from Patch and moved Tara out of the apartment on Lindell and into a better area. I didn't want her to rest her head where all the dirt was being done. I furnished her apartment in two days and kept the old apartment as a stash house for Patch and me.

We were in the middle of practice when the coach came over to me and said, "Your wife had went into labor and is at Fairview Hospital."

"What! I'd better get over there," I said, leaving the field in a hurry to a bunch of applauses and cheers.

When I got to the hospital, I was too late. Bonnie had already had the baby. She was lying on the bed holding the baby when I came into the room.

"Well, you got your wish."

"It's a boy," I said smiling. "I told you," I said, wagging my finger at her.

"Here. Hold him."

I grabbed him delicately and could see that he was going to have my nose and mouth.

"James. No matter what happens, promise me you will always be a father to your child."

"What make you ask me about that?"

"Just promise me."

"I promise," I said, looking into her eyes and then bending down and kissing her.

We named him Shane Harris, and they stayed in the hospital overnight. Of course, that night I went out and got drunk with Patch and a couple of the ball players. Besides Patch smacking a couple of dudes around in Déjà Vu, we had good time with Tara and a couple of the other strippers. I'm glad none of the dudes retaliated back because I didn't need no assault charge.

This was the first night I ever had sex with Tara inside the VIP section. She locked her legs around my waist and wouldn't let go until she was satisfied. She had the deejay play Janet Jackson's new song, "That's the Way Love Goes."

*****

Bonnie came through the door with Shane in her hands while I was still in the bed with a hangover.

I opened my eyes and saw her and said, "What time is it?"

"Too late for you to come and pick me up."

Now where did that sarcasm come from? I know in the beginning I seemed to be the uxorious type but not in this life will I be submissive to a woman. I love Bonnie, but we grew apart because of the time we were separated. But I'm the type of man that once I commit, I'm there through the good and the bad.

"I got drunk celebrating las' night," I said.

"I can see that much," she said, leaving the room with the baby.

The following weeks were all about the baby. She was putting a lot of attention into our son. I guess that was the only person she knew who wouldn't leave her all alone because I was always busy. I still had business to take care of that helped maintain her and the baby's lifestyle.

It was in mid-July when Patch came over my house and Bonnie was home. He was waiting for me and talking on his cell phone when Bonnie walked in the living room with Shane in her arms.

She came back upstairs and said, "Your friend is disrespectful."

"What did he do?" I said.

"He's talking on the phone using foul language while Shane and I are in the room."

"I'll go talk to him," I said while brushing my hair.

"I don't like him at all," Bonnie said.

Here we go again… I was used to hearing everybody say that about Patch. Even the guys didn't like his energy. When I got downstairs, Patch was just getting off the phone.

"Yo, Patch. My wife said you were talking foul on the phone in her presence."

"My fault, cuz. Ya' kno' I don't mean no harm by it, but this nigga is out of pocket in St. Paul."

"Is it serious?"

"Nothin' I can't handle," Patch said.

The next day when I went to go get a haircut at the shop, my barber was telling me that Patch just left out of here and smacked up the new barber named Eli and then pulled out his nine and took his jewelry. He claimed Eli's brother owed him money and was hiding from him and that he would get it out of Eli if he had to. Patch was not taking any shit. He was mean-spirited and hard on everybody he dealt with but me.

When preseason came, all I did was practice and work out hard. This was going to be my breakout year. I had one year option left, so I had to shine to ask for more money in the free agent field.

The Minnesota Vikings had picked up a running back in the draft from Ohio State the first round. He was just what we needed to help Chris Carter on offense. He looked good in the preseason games. I started drinking heavily during this time. Every Friday night, I bought a fifth of Jack Daniels. I would go to the strip clubs and drink even more and couldn't remember how I'd gotten home.

Bonnie would always be in bed already. I would get in bed beside her, and she would ignore me most of the time. But sometimes, she would give in to my touch. The next morning, she'd tell me that I needed to slow down wit' my drinking,

When the season started, I slowed down with the drinking and was having a Pro Bowl season. It was week six, and we were playing Green Bay Packers. I was up against a good offensive line. It was third down and five yards to go. The Packers were on their forty-yard line when Favre dropped back to pass, and I timed his throw perfectly for an interception. I started running down the field but was hit on my arm by a Packer. I knew I was going to lose the ball, but I saw my teammate, Roy Parker, on the side of me, so I fumbled the ball in his direction. Parker ran twenty-three yards for the first score of the game. I managed to get Brett Favre a couple more times and knocked down his passes. The offensive line for the Packers were catching penalties for being offside, trying to contain me. Roy Parker started pressuring Brett Favre from the other side. We finally got to him in the fourth quarter to seal the win.

By week seven, I had fifteen tackles and sacks. We were playing the Tampa Bay Buccaneers that weekend. I fell making a tackle. There was a pole on after the play, and one of the offensive linesmen from the Buccaneers fell on my foot. I was taken to the locker room on a stretcher and found out I had a broken right foot. I would be out the rest of the season.

I was a little depressed but more bored than ever. I started drinking on the weekends again. By Thanksgiving, I was drinking every day. I still took care of business with Patch too. It was much easier now too because I could board the team's plane with a suitcase full of drugs and money and not be searched. I was riding on the team's private jet.

It was Friday just before Christmas when I came home drunk from the barbershop. It was only 6:00 p.m. when I staggered in the house. Bonnie was on the sofa with Shane on her lap taking a nap.

She looked up at me, rolled her eyes, and said, "You need to tell your hoes to stop calling here."

"What yo' talkin' 'bout?" I said in my drunken slur.

"Some bitch named Judy keeps calling here. I thought you would've seen her by now. She's been calling all week. She had the nerve to tell me that she's your wife."

I started laughing and thinking about the fake wedding. Judy had started taking a few classes at Minnesota University and was probably calling for some money. I had not seen her since the first week in November.

"It's funny to you huh… I'm not putting up with this shit."

"What ya' gonna do?"

"I'm gonna leave your cheating drunken ass," she said, getting up with Shane.

His eyes were wide open and looking back and forth as Bonnie and I argued.

She put Shane down in the playpen and said, "You don't even have time for your son."

"Shut the fuck up! I pay the bills around here. I work my ass off fa' yo' to live good and take care of our son. You jus' spend up my money."

"So that means you can go out and fuck them bitches while I stay here in the house and wait for you to hop up and down on me whenever you ready?"

I walked over to her and slapped her across the face and then grabbed her by the shoulders and said, "You better watch ya' mouth."

"Keep off me! You'd better not put your hands on me!"

"You'll what?" I said, shaking the fear in her and pushing her to the sofa.

I left the house and went to hang out at the Rolex Strip Club. When I came back, it was eleven thirty, and the cops were waiting for me as I pulled up in front of the condo. I spent the Christmas weekend in jail. Bonnie ended up dropping the charges, but it was only the beginning of many fights to come.

When the New Year came, the season was over, and I couldn't go into the free agent field because of my injury. Bonnie had filed for a divorce and told the police that I was dangerous. She really wanted to tell them about my dealings with Patch, but I warned her a while ago that she would regret that the rest of her life.

My agent, Harold Lewis, assured me that he could get a deal off by trading me to Chicago or Cincinnati, but I didn't want to play for either of them. I decided to finish the last year of my contract in Minnesota.

The summer came and I worked hard on my foot injury. I stayed in the gym an average of four hours a day for five days a week. I still found time to hang out. Judy had moved back in with me. It was more convenient for my pockets and my insatiable sex life too.

I even started getting comfortable with Patch. I got bolder and started riding commercial flights with drugs from Texas to Minnesota. I figured, Why not? The police wouldn't expect me, a professional football player, to transport drugs. After minicamp, I delivered thirty bricks to Patch. He'd put it in the trunk of the Buick he'd rented, and we drove off in opposite directions.

The following morning, the phone rang at 6:00 a.m. on the nose.

I picked it up and said, "Hello," yawning.

"Yo, Harris. I need to talk to you," Patch said.

"It can't wait?" I said, whispering and trying not to wake Judy up.

"Nah. Meet at the spot. It's important."

"Aiight," I said, hanging the phone up quietly.

When I got to the apartment, Patch was already there. He had on a Champion hood, jeans, and a baseball cap pulled down on his head.

"Whut up, dirty," I said, coming through the door and closing it.

"Not a whole lotta good news. I got chased last night trying to get to St. Paul. I had to reroute and ended throwing the work away in the river."

"What!" I said trying to let what Patch said register. I sat down and looked him in the eyes for about thirty seconds and said, "Sixty-six pounds of coke. What happened?"

"I was being followed by a green Buick Skylark. The next thing I know, I seen another black sedan tailin' my ass. They were switching up, so when I had chance, I ditched them down by First and Lake and headed for the bridge by Manatawa River. I popped the trunk and threw the shit in the water."

"So did they catch ya'?"

"Hell nah. I left the rental on the road. Fuck that," Patch said. "The car wasn't in my name. Avis will find it when my folks report it missing."

I could tell he was telling the truth. What I had in mind was to lay low for a while.

I knew Patch wouldn't like that, so I said, "Don't worry about it. Let's keep our ears open."

I got back home a little after 3:00 p.m. Judy was still home.

"What you doin' here? No work today?"

"Nope. I got the mail this morning. There was something for a Mrs. Bonnie Harris. Who's that?"

I couldn't believe this. Judy have been looking through the mail.

"I was fidna' tell ya' I was married and had a divorce just before we were married, but I…"

"James. I know she was living here with you when I was gone. I'm not stupid. I love you. You're *mi rey*, but you don't treat me like a *reina*. Tell me the truth," Judy said with a calmness I knew was phony.

"Don't worry about it. It's all straightened out. Why don't you got to work?" I said, changing the subject.

"I got my schedule changed to part-time. And I was raised to honor and respect my husband. It's wrong to talk disrespectful to your husband, so I'm going to always respect you no matter what. I hope you can do the same," Judy said, walking up the stairs.

When the season started, I was ready. What I wasn't ready for was the divorce settlement. I was glad Bonnie wasn't vindictive, but I had to pay alimony of five thousand a month. There was no way one year and a woman would need that amount of money. But I had no problem paying it. As a matter of fact, I never missed a payment.

I had stopped hustling completely now in Minnesota because the police were suspicious of me. They were pulling me over on a regular basis and telling me I needed to watch my company. Patch was on the run from the Feds. He was either in hiding or back in Cali. It wasn't until the first week of December when I was home looking at the news that I knew where Patch was. He was found dead right around the corner from the stash house on 25th Street. One nine-millimeter bullet was found in his neck. He was shot up close. The body was identified by an unknown relative and was being sent back to California. I called Tara and she knew about Patch already. Word on the street was he had too many enemies for anyone to pinpoint one person who could have done it.

That same weekend, I went out to the strip club with a rookie on the team named Todd. He wanted to go to Déjà Vu with me and get him the royal treatment he heard the other players were talking about that I'd been getting them. Since we had a home game on Sunday night against the Lions, I decided to take him there Friday night. When we got in the club, we went straight to the VIP section. Tara came right up there.

"Hey, James," she said, sitting on my lap.

"Whassup, girl. I jus' came ta' check on ya' and my man right there wants the royal treatment," I said in her ear.

"Aiight, I'll go tell the girls, but I'm not coming right back. I'll be up here later," she said, getting off my lap.

I patted her on the ass as she got up and walked off.

A little while later, about five dancers came up to the VIP. I knew all of them except for two. They were new girls. I found out their names were Gia and Beauty. Beauty was White girl trapped in a Black girl's body. Her ass was like a sister. She had petite-sized breasts and an innocent look that would fool a priest. Gia looked more weathered. She was drinking up all the champagne and was very pushy. What she lacked in beauty, she made up by being sexy with nice long legs and pretty lips. She made a mole on her lip that made her appear vogue. As they kept dancing and drinking, we tipped them all well, but like I said, Gia was too pushy. She was trying to tell the other girls what to do, so I ignored her. My partner Todd did the same. Beauty gave me a lap dance while Gia sat on the side of me looking upset. The next thing I knew, the champagne glass hit my face.

I grabbed my face and saw blood leaking onto my hands and my tailor-made sweater. When I looked up, I saw her strutting off, so I reached out and grabbed her like a Road Doll. I ran her body up and down the bar table, holding her neck until her face had so much blood on it that I couldn't see her eyes.

When I threw her to the floor, Todd ran over and kicked her with his gator boots and said, "Bitch, you done fucked up now."

After a few more kicks to her stomach, he came over to me and said, "Let me see your face."

"I'm aiight," I said, pushing him away.

"Hell no. That shit's leaking. C'mon," Todd said, leading the way out of VIP.

The bouncers stopped us, looked at my face, and wanted to know what happened. Before I knew it, the manager was in front of me along with Tara, who grabbed my arm and never left my side. The other strippers told the manager what happened while Todd and I were leaving. They got Gia and told her she had to leave and never come back.

Todd walked me to my Range, and I said, "Go home. I'll be aiight."

"You sure?"

"Yeah, man," I said, getting into the jeep.

I got seventeen stitches put right up under my right eye. My cheekbone was sore the next morning, but I managed to get up and go to practice on Saturday morning. When I walked on the field, I could still smell the alcohol coming from my body.

"Damn! What happened to you?" Willie Shaw said.

"I got hit in the face with a beer bottle yesterday in the club."

"Man, go in the office and show the coach. I don't need you to practice today looking like that," he said, shaking his head in disgust.

The defensive back coach had become like a father to me since I got on the team. He could tell I had been drinking.

When I got to the office, Coach Green was just getting off the phone.

"Good Lord! What happened to you?" Coach Green said with concern on his face when he saw my face.

I told him that I was playing pool in the club, and a woman was standing behind me when my pool stick poked her between the legs. Then she turned around and hit me with her drink and cut my face. Coach sent me home immediately.

I woke up the next morning and my face was throbbing. Judy was staring at my face while lying beside me. She'd gotten off work late last night. I'd told her my face was an accident at football practice yesterday.

The next day, I got to the stadium to warm up with the team and took painkillers. I felt a whole lot better but didn't play that much. The defensive coach wanted to save me for the playoffs. "You could play hurt, but you can't play injured" was my theory, but whenever Coach Shaw spoke, I listened. He knew what he was talking about. At the time, Detroit wasn't a factor anyway. Barry Sanders had a big game, but we won by a field goal.

The following week, I had the stitches removed and cosmetic surgery to remove the scar. It looked as if nothing had happened to my face.

We had made the playoffs once again but had to play the Bears. They gave us a difficult time whenever we played them. The game was on our turf, so we felt confident we could outscore them, but they came out with their offensive working on all cylinders. The final score was 35-18 with the Bears winning.

The season was over, and I had my agent work on trading me to another team immediately. I really wanted to play for the Rams. It was boring in Minnesota. I was ready to leave.

I started going to the Timber Wolves' games and hanging out with a couple of the players. They were younger than me but had a sense of humor and were always looking for a good time. One of the players, J. R. Ride, would bring his boys down from Oakland to hang out in Minnesota. We would go to Vegas or play Madden NFL on Sega at J. R.'s house. I went to St. Paul with J. R. He liked to go to the Lamplighter. It wasn't all that sophisticated. It was raunchy if you ask me, but I liked it too. It reminded me of back home.

We stepped in and were heading toward their little VIP section when I saw Gia.

"Hey! Come here," I said, feeling good off a fifth of Hennessey we drank on the way there. "I'm not gonna do nothin' to ya'... Come here," I said.

Gia finally came and said, "Whassup, James. I never got a chance to apologize."

"Apologize?" I said, knitting my brows and looking down at her.

"Yeah. That was my mistake. I meant to throw the drink in your face, but my arm went too close... I'm sorry about that."

I looked at her and thought about it for a second. It sounded like the truth. "How long you've been here?"

"A couple of weeks. Is that J. R. and the click you with?"

"Yeah. Why?"

"I didn't know you knew them. You going up to VIP?"

"Yeah," I said nodding my head.

"I'm coming up there to give you a freebie," she said, strutting off quickly with just a sheer robe over a skimpy red outfit.

I could tell J. R. was a regular. All the girls knew him. I couldn't believe Gia's hospitality. She gave me two free lap dances, and they were top choice.

After the second one, she said, "James," and reached inside my pants and squeezed my semihard dick.

"What you wanna do?" I said, looking into her eyes.

I didn't have to say no more. She got on her knees and began unzipping my pants. She even put a body bag on it and rode me reverse-cowgirl style. Gia made up for the looks with the sex appeal and skills. She felt like she had suction cups around my manhood. She had serious muscle control.

By June, my agent Harold had cut a deal with the Vikings for another two years. We didn't even make the playoff in "95." During the off-season, my wish came true. Harold made the Vikings pursue a deal to trade me for a future draft pick to the Rams. Judy was upset that I was changing teams because she was comfortable going to school in Minnesota, and her airport job made adjustments for her already.

I sold all my furniture in the condo and the stash house. What surprised me was that they never bothered to count the money in both safes. It was 1.5 million dollars in cash altogether. I had two months left on the lease, so I decided to come back and get the money later.

It was April when I had purchased a house in West County. It was in Creek Courts. I flew back to Minnesota to get my money out of the apartment because I was through with Minnesota. I decided to take the bus back to St. Louis because it was safer to travel on the bus with a large suitcase, but it had mysteriously disappeared. I searched all over the bus and every piece of luggage on the bus. I couldn't believe it. I let 1.5 million dollars get taken from me right before my eyes.

Chapter 9

Home Sweet Home

Poverty is a disease of the mind.

—S. B. Fuller

Now that I was close to home, I felt a whole lot better. Judy had decided to stay in Minnesota, so she can finish school. She was sharing an apartment with Leandra but would come to St. Louis almost every weekend to be with me. That wasn't a bad arrangement. I was in East St. Louis most of the time with family and friends who I never took the time to introduce Judy to.

The neighborhood was the same, but the people were changing. There were a lot of kids living in poverty, and I wanted to do something about it. As a child, growing up, I knew that being poor started at an early age in my mind. For example, if your friends had better clothes or better living conditions than you, nobody had to tell you this. You could tell them. Fats, T. I., and I made sure if someone had something, so did the others, but unity is not something a lot of poor people are used to.

I decided to get ahold of my lawyer and looked into government-funded programs the city had for the poor and disenfranchised. I found out about a fund called TIFF. Then I came up with a project and named it Families of America (FA). This program was about building better homes for the low-income families. I mapped out a blueprint with my lawyer and gave it to the East St. Louis city manager named Mr. Henderson.

When the preseason started, I was in good spirits and good shape, which led me to play good ball. Now I was looking at the game in yards instead of downs. I was taking any downs off. I was determined to get to the quarterback and stop the running fame of any opposing offense. I figured if our defense could stop a team's offense from gaining over a hundred yards running and two hundred yards passing, we'd win a lot of games.

The last preseason game, my son Kyle came to see me along with my brother Eric and my cousin Earl. Me and Earl were the same age and could pass for brothers. He was always getting in some kind of trouble since he was a juvenile. This was the first time I'd seen him since leaving college because every time I came back, he was either on the run or in jail.

After the game was over against the Cleveland Browns, I showered and made my way out to the parking lot to see my family. My son Kyle was ten years old and getting big.

He smiled as he saw me coming and said, "Hey, Dad! Number 99 was looking good on the team."

I rubbed his head and said, "Yeah. You were watching me closely, huh?"

"Yup," Kyle said with his one-of-a-kind laugh and giggle.

"Yeah. Ya' look good, kinfolk," Earl said, holding his arms up in the air.

I walked over and we hugged each other.

"Whassup, kinfolk. Ya' gonna stay outta trouble now?"

"Man, I gotta get mine," Eric said with a smile.

"That we do know," Eric said, adding his two cents to the conversation.

"C'mon ya'll. I'm fit'na take us to somethin' to eat," I said, walking over to the Benz.

"Daddy, can I ride with you?"

"Of course," I said, turning back and seeing Eric open the door to his white Bronco.

We went and ate in Belleville, Illinois, at a restaurant called Eli's. All of us ordered steaks and home fries along with salads and apple pies. As we were waiting for our food, a guy I grew up with came in to eat with a woman.

"Hey, James!"

"Whassup, Ron."

"Long time no see. I heard you back in town now."

"Yeah," I said, nodding my head at the chocolate-complexion thick woman he was with.

"This is Jessica. Meet James, Eric, Earl…and who is this?

"My son, Kyle."

"Ooh…okay," Ron said, shaking my son's hand.

Jessica said, "Glad to meet y'all," and then stood by Ron's side holding his hand.

"What brings y'all over here?"

"Ya' kno' we like to come over here to get out eatn' on," Earl said.

"Yeah. Well Eli is lookn' for a buyer. He told me this a few months ago. He was fid'na put a sign in the window? Thinks it'll run business way."

"Oh yeah," I said, smiling and shaking my head.

"Yeah. I'm thinking about buying it, but I need a little more cash. I'll see y'all around," Ron said, heading for a table with Jessica trailing and turning heads.

Her walk was making her ass do a rendition of hoetry in motion in a high skirt.

Our food came, and as we talked and made up for lost time, I was thinking about what Ron said. I wondered how much the restaurant was selling for.

I took Kyle home and then went home and changed out of jeans to my tailor-made silk pants and shirt. Eric, Earl, and I decided to go to the boat. I went and picked them up in the Range Rover, and my brother had on Versace hookup with blue gators, and Earl had on crème-colored silk shirt and some dress pants to match along with some Florsheims.

We went straight to the blackjack table. I was getting my drink on but felt like I was being watched the whole time. Now I don't have ophthalmophoria but my sixth sense was telling me somewhere in the casino, somebody was eyeballing me hard.

It wasn't until we were clocking that I noticed her staring at me from a distance. I made my way over to her as we were walking to leave the boat.

"Whassup, Corry."

"Hey, James," she said, waving her hand.

She was with two of her girls, and they were staring at me. They both looked familiar.

"Courtney, where y'all going?" Eric said.

"To the casino," she said, popping the gum in her mouth.

It all came to me. Courtney and Amy were the other two. They were four years younger than me. Now they were all grown up and… Corr…I could always tell her apart from her twin sister, Torry. Corry was older by two minutes, but Torry was the outgoing one. Corry was the quiet and shy one. They both wore their hair in bobs and stayed away from the extension and makeup.

"What ya' doin' out here?"

"I always come out here. My sister works here."

"Yeah. Where's Torry at?"

"She probably at the casino," she said, falling back to talk to me as we walked off the boat.

Courtney and Amy were with Eric and Earl in front of us.

"You haven't called since the beginning of the summer."

"Yeah. I've been busy. I ain't forgot ya'," I said, looking down into her pretty brown eyes.

"I can't tell. I'll come check ya' tomorrow."

"You promise?" I said.

"C'mon, Corry!" Courtney was yelling.

"See ya' later," she said as she walked away quickly in her heels and skirt.

I watched her legs as she walked away. Damn, she looked even better than I remembered!

The following Sunday morning, I was awakened in bed by Judy. She had dropped by unexpectedly as usual and climbed in bed with me. She put her face in my lap and wouldn't come up for air until I pulled her up by her hair.

"What are doing, girl?"

"I miss *mi rey*. You don't miss your *reina*?"

"Yeah," I said with a smile.

"Good. Now let me handle this," Judy said, straddling my waist and inserting me inside her.

I laid back and just watched her go to work. Judy had a strong sex drive and looked fine even when she was cumming. What I like the most about her was her accent. She sounded good talking Spanish. It turned me on. We stayed in the house all day and enjoyed the indoor swimming pool. At night, we ordered some pizza and went into the entertainment room to watch a movie. The next day, Judy left around noon.

I drove to East St. Louis and got there a little after 4:00 p.m. I picked up the care phone and called Corry's house and told her I was on my way over.

When I got there, Torry answered the door and said, "What took you so long?"

"Don't even try it. You ain't Corry."

"I see you can't be fooled still," Torry said, laughing real loud.

"Nope. I know y'all too well," I said, walking inside the living room.

It was well furnished with family pictures all around the room. Trophies were in the china cabinet. I knew they were Torry's because she used to be a tomboy.

"Long time no see. You act like you don't have time to stop by," Torry said, punching me in the shoulder.

"Aiight, girl. I was fit'na punch ya' back."

"And I'll sue you," Torry said, laughing that loud laugh again.

Corry came down the stairs in a Guess T-shirt and jeans looking better than the other day without makeup on.

"What y'all down here doin'?"

"Nuttin'. Just playin'," Torry said.

"Whassup, girl," I said, walking over to Corry and kissing her on the cheek.

"Hmmm…you smell good."

"I jus' better. I jus' come out the shower."

"Well, I got to leave you two lovebirds for work," Torry said.

"I heard you working at the boat."

"Yeah. I'll see you later, James," Torry said, leaving out the door.

"So what's been up wit' ya'?"

"Nothin'. Just workin' at the factory downtown."

"No man to keep ya' busy?"

"Nope," Corry said, slightly blushing.

"Where your moms at?"

"She's at work. She'll be home in a coupl'a hours. You thirsty?"

"Yeah. What you got?"

"Let's go see," she said, leading the way to the kitchen.

We decided to drink some lemonade and eat a piece of chocolate cake that was in the kitchen. We took it out on the porch and saw some girls outside playing double Dutch while the boys were riding their bikes up and down the block. We talked about what everybody was doing around the neighborhood until I heard the ice cream truck coming down the block.

"I gotta buy those kids some ice cream."

"What about me?"

"What you want?"

"A strawberry sundae," she said.

I stopped the ice cream truck and rounded up all the kids. It was a total of eight at first and then many more came from out of nowhere. I didn't know so many children were on the block.

After I finished buying all the kids ice cream, I went back on the porch with Corry to eat our ice cream. Two little girls followed me and stopped right in front of us, licking their vanilla cones.

"Hey, Keisha and Teisha," Corry said, waving to them.

"Hi, Corry," they said in unison.

"Who's them thurr children?" I asked.

"You remember Ashley, right? Well, she's on that shit and got her grandmother watching her kids," Corry said.

I looked at the little girls and instantly felt sorry for them. "Who's the daddy?"

"That boy named Maurice. He got outta the Feds a little while ago."

"You mean Li'l Darryl's cousin?"

"Yeah. He's trifflin' too. He don't mind them like he's s'ppose to."

I looked at Keisha and Teisha and said, "How old are you two?"

"I'm nine," Keisha said.

"I'm six," Teisha said, exposing a missing front tooth.

"You'll better go back and play now," Corry said.

"Okay. Thank you," they both said before running off.

"Damn! Their clothes look bad."

"I know! That's their fa' real clothes they send them off to school wit'," Corry said.

I shook my head and said, "We are going to take them shopping this weekend."

"Fa' real, James?"

"Of course. I don't like to see that right thurr," I said, shaking my head.

Corry sat on my lap and kissed me on the lips and said, "You got a good heart."

I knew Sunday was our home opener, so I planned the shopping for early Saturday morning. Corry had the girls at her house when I got there. She said their grandmother was so happy. She kept saying, "God bless you."

We went to the mall, and I bought them five pairs of named branded jeans a piece along with some blouses and two dresses each for them to go to church in. Of course, I got them some girls' Jordans and then I took them to McDonald's. Keisha and Teisha ordered Big Macs and fries too. We ate like a family inside the restaurant.

The little girls were talking little girl talk while I told Corry about my plans for East St. Louis. She was just smiling while listening to me. Then I told her about Judy Krude and the fake marriage ceremony I did with Li'l Darryl posing as a reverend. Corry couldn't stop laughing. All the way back home, she was still laughing and saying, "I don't believe you did that, and she was stupid enough not to know better."

I wanted to take Corry home with me, but I knew I had a game tomorrow. Besides, when I got home, Judy could be there.

Chapter 10

The Setup

A deceitful man will always find plenty who are ready to be deceived.

—Niccolo Machiavelli

The season wasn't looking too prosperous. It was the month of October and week six was coming up in the NFL. We only had win. I was glad the bye week was coming up. We had gotten picked apart by the San Francisco 49ers on Sunday, and as we rode the team jet back to St. Louis, everybody was quiet except for Mr. Norv Turner.

"You should be ashamed of yourselves! Not for losing but for giving up! You have to play as hard as you can," he said.

We all just listened. Some of the players were nursing injuries while others acted like they were tired. When I got home that night, I was surprised to see a letter on the coffee table from Bonnie. When I opened it, there were pictures of my son Shane. I was looking at the resemblance of me when Judy walked in the room.

"I thought I heard you come in," she said, walking toward me in a teddy with her heels on.

Judy knew this was my favorite outfit. I just wasn't in the mood for her. I'd promised myself that I would spend this week with Corry, and that was all I wanted to do.

"Yeah. You brought the mail in?"

"Uh-huh. I thought you'd be home in the morning."
"We flew back right after the game."
"You got pictures?"
"Yeah. This is my son Shane."
"Your second. Where's your first?"
"He lives in East St. Louis. I had him when I was in high school."
"There's a lot of secrets you're keeping from me," Judy said, walking back up the stairs to the bedroom.

I didn't even respond to her last comment. I shouldn't have ever, ever told her about Kyle. It had slipped out. I've been with Judy for over a year, and all we do is have sex. But I can't deny that it is good. I went up to the bedroom and found her lying down looking at the television.

"Why haven't you gotten pregnant by me?"

She glared at me and said, "For your information, I'm on the pill. If you would pay more attention to me, you would've known that."

"You should've told me that. When you plan on getting off the pill?"

"When I finish school. I got one more semester. Look, James…I don't want to argue. I gotta leave tomorrow. Just come to bed," Judy said, pouting her lips and trying to change the tense atmosphere.

I'm not one to hold a grudge with a fine half-naked woman, so I removed my clothes, took a quick shower, and got into bed. Judy was all over me with her tongue. She was shrimping and tea bagging me when she stuck her tongue in my butt. That did it, I was ready for action.

*****

When I pulled up in front of Corry's house, Keisha and Teisha ran over to my car.

"Hey, Keisha and Teisha," I said as they grabbed my pants leg.

They were both wearing the Guess outfit and Jordan sneakers I'd bought them.

"Godfather, where you going?" they said in unison, not forgetting what I told them they could call me.

"To see Corry," I said, pushing Teisha off my leg just enough for me to walk.

Before I could get into the house, Corry came to the door.

"I could hear them from up in my room calling you," she said.

I just smiled at the two little girls who I were taking a big liking to.

"Y'all go play. I ain't goin' nowhere."

"You promise you'll buy us some ice cream?" Teisha asked.

"Yeah, I promise."

"Okay," Teisha said, smiling and showing that missing tooth before running off to go play.

It was an Indian summer for October. Kids were able to come outside and play without jackets.

Corry was at the door looking at me and said, "Them girls gonna worry you ta' death."

"Let 'em. I don't mind."

"Well, I do. Let their daddy take care of 'em."

"Damn! Where that come from?"

"Jus' come inside," Corry said.

She had the stereo on and was playing a Toni Braxton CD. The song "Seven Whole Days" was filing the air as Corry walked to the sofa with some chino-type pants on.

"Where you goin'?"

"I gotta go to work at six."

"Why didn't you tell me?"

"I didn't know you were comin' over this late in the day. I'm sorry," she said.

"I'll drive you down there," I said, looking at my watch.

"It don't take long to go downtown. We got an hour or so."

"If you say so," I said, sitting down on the sofa.

She sat down next to me and started talking about when we should go out on a real date. While we talked, I flirted with her and found out Corry wasn't only shy but didn't have confidence in herself. She wanted me to decide everything. Where we should go, what we should do. She wouldn't put any input into our date.

After a while, I heard the ice cream truck, and Corry reminded me about my promises. I went outside and bought the whole neighborhood ice cream. By the time I finished, my cousin and Fathead were coming down the block.

"Hey, kinfolk. Whassup wit'chu. Look who I got wit'me," Fats said.

"Yeah, cuz. I been lookin' all over for ya'," Earl said.

I could smell the Michelob on his breath. I looked him straight in the eyes and saw he wasn't drunk or high, so I said, "Whassup? Talk to me."

He got out of the Cadillac and started walking away from the car.

I took a few steps away from Fats' car and said, "Man, you can talk right here."

"Aiight, cuz. Check it out. I want to do somethin' big. Niggaz ain't consistent on the Southside, and I want to move some work. You kno' who I'm 'round here. I'll mek it happen round her're. you kno' what I'm sayin'."

"Aiight, kinfolk. We'll make it happen, but we'll kick it later. I'm fid'na do somethin'."

"Aiight, cuz. I'll get back at ya'. I got ya' cell phone number," Earl said, walking back to the car.

"Ayo, Fathead, whassup?"

"Ain't shit. What up too?"

"I'm 'bout to take Corry to work."

"Aiight. Meet me up aft the Max tonight."

"That's a bet," I said, giving them both a handshake before they drove off.

Corry came out of the house ready to go to work She looked at me and said, "I heard what you told them girls."

"What?" I said, trying to play like I couldn't remember.

"That you'll take them swimming at your house in a big swimming pool," Corry said, rolling her eyes.

"Yeah. You're coming too. Do you work Saturdays?"

"No."
"Aiight. It's on."

*****

Right after practice, I went and got me some Kyle and then went and got Corry. She then went to get Keisha and Teisha. I drove the Range Rover so the kids could have a lot of room in the back. I drove them to my house with the Biggie Smalls CD, playing "Ready to Die."

When I pulled up in the garage, I could hear Keisha and Teisha getting excited. "Our godfather is rich," they were saying.

We all got out the ride and went inside. I gave Corry the tour around the house while Kyle took the girls straight to the swimming pool.

After I showed Corry the four bedrooms, she said, "You got a big house for just the two of you."

"You mean one."

"What about your wife?" she said laughing.

"You on joke time now," I said, smiling and pushing her on the bed. I fell on top of her and started sucking on her neck.

"Hmmm, James. Not now. We got to go downstairs with the kids in the swimming pool."

I stopped and pulled her up off the bed and said, "Let's go."

We all got into the swimming pool and began to play around. Keisha and Teisha were getting along just fine. Corry was having fun too. She was wearing a bronze-colored one-piece bathing suit that matched her skin tone. I watched her in fascination playing with the kids when I came back from the bathroom. She was laughing and having a good time. The hours flew by, and it started getting dark.

Corry emerged out of the water then came over where I was seated.

"What you got to eat?" she asked, wrapping her head with a towel.

"There's a lot of food up in the kitchen," I said, looking at her body.

She started blushing and said, "Stop staring at me."

"Why? I know you like it."
"I do?"
"Yup," I said, smiling at her.
"Let's get the kids out of the water before we go in the kitchen. I don't want nothing to happen to any of them," she said, sitting down on one of the recliners that was by the pool.

I called for all of them to go eat, and they raced out of the pool into the living room and started dripping water on my three-inch thick crush velvet carpet.

"You'll get back out there and sue them towels to dry off," I said, coming in behind them.

Still dressed in our swimwear, Corry and I went in the kitchen and took out some turkey lunch meat and Swiss cheese. Anything else would have taken too long. We quickly sliced up the meat and cheese and then got a big bag of microwavable popcorn and put it out for everybody to eat.

"I didn't know you could cook," Corry said, standing beside me and laughing.

"Oh. You got jokes," I said, hearing the door slam in the house.

I could tell no one else heard it, but I knew my house. A minute later, Judy emerged in the kitchen looking at everyone.

"I thought I heard somebody in the kitchen." She was standing in the doorway with her hands on her hips.

I watched Corry eye her from head to toe and saw a disgusted look come across her face. She didn't like Judy at first sight. Judy was smaller but higher maintenance than Corry. Looking at them both, you see the difference in attitudes right away because Judy exuded confidence, and Corry was a little intimidated by her presence.

She sat down at the table among the children when Judy walked over to me and said, "Hola, *mi rey*."

"Whassup," I said, looking her straight in the eyes. When I looked at the kids and saw they were eating with no other care in the world, I said, "Judy, I want to introduce you to Corry. That's my son Kyle and my goddaughters Keisha and Teisha."

After Judy spoke to all of them, I excused us from the kitchen and went up to the bedroom with her.

As soon as we got up there, Judy said, "I hope that's one of your baby's mommas because—"

"Because what?" I said, cutting her off.

"Because if it's not, that's disrespectful."

"It's not."

"Who is she then?"

"None of your business."

"Oh. It's like that now. That's how you playing me?"

I could tell where this was leading to. Judy always threw it up in my face that she was my wife. She was about to graduate with a degree in human resources but wasn't smart enough to realize our marriage was bogus.

I reminded myself I had to change the locks and said, "Listen, I ain't trying to argue with you. All them people is my family."

"I'm your wife and you won't even introduce me to your *familia*," she said with tears in her eyes.

"When you take time out of your schedule, maybe I will."

"I'll make time for that," she said, plopping down on the bed, taking her pumps off and knee-high stockings.

"Are they spending the night?"

"No. I'm about to take them back," I said, leaving the bedroom.

I drove everybody back home before Judy came back downstairs and wanted to meet them. Corry wasn't acting the same as I drove back to East St. Louis. I dropped Kyle off first. Then I dropped the girls off and watched them go inside their home.

"I could walk from here," Corry said.

"Why you wanna do that?" I said.

"Good night, James," Corry said, getting out of the ride and walking toward her house.

I stopped by my mother's house for a while, and she told me that my grandmother wanted to see me, so I decided to go see her tomorrow.

As I headed for home, I stopped for gas on Broadway at the Clark Gas Station. When I pulled up, it looked as if nobody was around but then I noticed an old Buick across the street. I went inside to pay for my gas at the window and then came out to pump my gas. To be on the safe side, I stood as if I had a gun because this was a dangerous zone at night. When I finished pumping the gas and pulled out, I noticed the old Buick's car lights came on, and it started following behind me. I decided to reroute and go to the Max.

I pulled up in front of the Max and parked quickly. When I was going inside, I saw the old Buick stop by my ride and then parked about ten yards away from it. When they got the car, I got a glimpse of what they had on and then went inside. Just my luck if they were trying to rob and kill me.

As I made my way to the back of the club where they were gambling, I saw Fats, T. I., my cousin Earl, and Li'l Darryl standing around the table.

"Yo! You'll ain't gonna believe this," I said, stopping the crap game.

"Try us," Fats said, holding the dice.

"Two muthafuckas followed me up in here."

"Where they?" Earl said, picking his money off the table and heading for the door.

Everybody followed behind him looking around the club.

I spotted them at the bar with their backs turned and said, "There they go by the bar."

"Aiight. I'm fid'na tell Big Gary its goin' down in here. He'll back us fa' sure because it's you," Fats said.

I went to Gary's office with Fats, and I told him the story. He immediately put his men on the door and stopped all traffic coming in. He then started letting some people leave. When the two dudes tried leaving, four of Gary's men held them inside, pulling out their guns. Big Gary put on all the lights, and I came out first with the crew behind me.

"This who ya' lookin' fa'?" Earl said, pointing at me.

The two men looked as if they saw ghosts.

"Tie 'em up to the chairs," T. I. said, throwing some rope on the floor in front us.

They were tied back-to-back in two chairs. I could see they were young. They started pleading not to be hurt because they didn't do anything. Then they eventually confessed when they knew they were not being let go; they followed me because of the chain they saw around my neck. They swore they didn't know it was me, but that didn't stop the torture and ass whipping. They were both pistol-whipped and beat with baseball bats on their bodies before being let go. Although there weren't any facial injuries or blood, they were in excruciating pain and glad to be alive. T. I. took their car keys and searched the car with another guy named Ro and found two nine-millimeters. They kept the guns, and we threw one dude in the front seat, the other in the back of the car. They were all broken up, but somehow, they got to the hospital without any assistance from us. That's when I decided not to wear any more chains or rings.

I stayed in the Max and kicked it with my friends. Big Gary opened back the doors, and we got drunk. I gave my cousin the chain to keep and told him I'd have fifty thousand to him before next weekend.

I woke up the following morning on my grandmother's sofa a little after 11:00 a.m. She went to church already, but I remember her saying that she wanted me to adjust the floor model television because the picture was messing up, and she wanted to look at the soap operas. I got up and took a cold shower first. Then I made an omelet and fried some bacon. After drinking some orange juice and lots of water, I was ready to function. I fixed the television and watched the Bears playing. I wondered why my grandmother wouldn't just let me buy her a new TV. I got into the game after washing the dishes when someone rang the doorbell. I saw the truck through the window and knew who it was.

"Whassup, li'l bro," I said, opening the door.

"Whassup wit'chu? I heard what went down last night at the Max," Eric said.

"Yeah. It's all straightened out. Young-ass niggaz didn't kno' no better."

"I kno' dem niggaz. They from Arkansas originally. They moved down here a coupl'a years ago and been taxing muthafukas. They roll wit' tha blood set."

"Yeah. Well, they fucked wit' tha wrong muthafucka," I said.

"I kno' that's right. Where's Grandma? At church?"

"Yeah. You fid'na wait 'round for her?"

"I don't kno'. Why?"

"She told me she wanna holla at ya'. I'll wait around wit'chu," I said, turning my attention back to the game.

It was close to 4:00 p.m. when my grandmother came back. She came in the house with one of her friends named Joyce. Joyce remembered when we were babies. She said she looks at football and watches me play. She even knew my jersey number. I stayed in the living room with Joyce while Grandma and Eric were in the kitchen. After fifteen minutes of us talking, Grandma called me in the kitchen and sent Eric in the living room.

"Sit down at the table," she said.

I sat down and looked at my grandma; she still was the leader of the family and didn't look her age at all.

"Now you kno' I'm proud of you. But you gotta look after ya' li'l brotha. He startin' to hang with the wrong heap of boys. Jus' spend some time wit' him, son."

"I'll try, Grandma, but you kno' how it is. He's always on the move when I come around."

"Make time for him. He looks up to you. I bet he wouldn't be over here now if it wasn't for you."

"You right," I said, getting up and kissing her on the cheek. "I fixed the television too. I gotta go home."

"Aiight, son. Jus' remember what I said," she said, standing up.

"I will," I said, leading the way to the living room and telling Joyce good night.

Eric and I went our separate ways. I went to go see Corry. To my surprise, both she and her sister Torry were home. I sat on the couch looking at football while Corry was making some iced tea to drink.

Torry sat down next to me and said, "We heard what happened at the Max."

"Yeah. Who told ya?"

"Our girls called us early today. You kno' how news travel."

"Yeah, Telegram, telephone, tell-a-nigga," I said.

Torry was laughing as Corry came in the room with a tray of iced tea and glasses. They sat and listened to me tell them everything that happened last night. We talked for a while. Then the phone rang for Torry, and she got up and left us alone.

"You aiight?"

"I should be askin' you that after last night."

"You kno' what I mean. Listen…I'm 'bout to kick her ass out and change the locks."

"And what that s'ppose to mean?"

"I want us together."

Corry ran her hands through her hair and said, "Let me think about it."

"There's nothing to think about."

"Yes, it is. You're rich and famous. I'm—"

"You're the woman I want to be with," I said, reaching over and kissing her.

Corry didn't resist. I didn't want to go all the way, so I stopped. Her eyes were dancing as I stood up.

"I gotta go. I'll see you later," I said.

She walked me to the door, and we kissed again. She put her hand between my legs.

When we stopped, she said, "Come over early tomorrow before I go to work."

After is said I would, I went to get in the Range Rover when a police car pulled up on the side of me. It was Fred the cop.

"James. I knew that was your ride. What's goin' on?"

"Nothin' much. Just visiting some friends," I said smiling.

"Yeah. Let me have a word wit'chu for a minute."

I walked over to the police car, and he said, "I heard what went down yesterday. I want you to know I got back. I went to see them punks this morning and told them there will be serious repercussions if something happens to you on the sly."

"Yeah. Thanks but everything's cool."

"Jus' makin' sure. I'll see ya' round," Fred said, driving off.

The following days went fast. I had practice to attend on Monday morning and couldn't see Cory. Tuesday morning, my lawyer called me and told me Mr. Henderson got everything set up for the project. He had the papers for me to sign, and I could write a check for one million dollars to get everything started. So I got my checkbook out, and I did just that. I decided to take fifty thousand to my cousin after Thursday's practice.

When game day came on Sunday, I felt good. My conscience was feeling like I was making all the right decisions. We even won the game coming off the bye week.

By the time Thanksgiving came around, I hadn't seen Earl. He was ducking and dodging me. Everybody knew about me giving him some money and jewelry. I decided to forget about him. He would need me again. He was nothing but a con man at heart.

By Christmas, the Rams season was over with. We didn't make the playoffs. I decided to go get more involved into Families of America (FA). That's when I found out the project wasn't even off the ground. My lawyer, Mr. Henderson, and I sat in an office in City Hall, and Mr. Henderson explained everything to me. Kevin Ellis had a major role in the project. He was the man of regulatory affairs. He was the man who initially took the check I had signed for a million dollars. I needed to meet this man face-to-face.

Chapter 11

The Con

But if I am apparently crushed by the system of influence and misdirected power, my cause shall rise again to plague the conscience of the corrupt.

—Marcus Garvey

After my lawyer and I had a few meetings with Mr. Henderson and Kevin Ellis, we all decided to go ahead with the plans on building Families of America. In March, I went to City Hall to hear how the community leaders felt. Mrs. Shavers, the block association leader, was one of the speakers along with Kevin Ellis, Mr. Henderson, and few others.

Mrs. Shavers was a lady who was born, raised, and married in East St. Louis. Her husband had died a few years ago. Her family came from Mississippi. She had four kids, and they had kids who all lived in East St. Louis and didn't plan on leaving. She was all for the FA project and had a list of signatures that were also for it. She spoke as if she was a reverend doing a sermon. She put Kevin Ellis on a pedestal when she recited Psalms 1:3 in honor of him. I just watched with admiration and wondered why my name wasn't mentioned about contributing a million dollars as of yet. As the hearing came to a close, Kevin Elis walked over to me and shook my hand. He was wearing a Hart Schaffner and Mark three-piece suit. I looked at him and wondered if he could afford this on his salary as a regulatory of affairs.

"Congratulations, Mr. Harris. You're the one that only really make this happen," he said, smiling and showing off his capped teeth.

"Yeah, but you're the one that has to get approved," I said.

"Don't worry. It's as good as done. In a couple of months, you can find a construction crew, and we can start putting buildings on the land."

"I'm glad because sooner than later, that land would've been used for something else."

"Yeah. I think you're right. I hope you're not in a rush. Come to the office so we can talk a little more," Mr. Ellis said.

"I will," I said as he walked away.

There were a lot of reporters taking pictures. I managed to take a few pictures with Mr. Ellis and Mr. Henderson. Then it was off to Mr. Ellis' office. All three of us went. Mr. Ellis surprised me and pulled out a bottle of Louis XIV Cognac.

"Do you drink?" he asked me.

"Yeah," I said, looking at the bottle and wondering if it was a gift or purchase.

Mr. Ellis pulled out three drinking glasses from his desk and opened the bottle. He methodically poured all of us a glass, muttering rhetorically about how he felt good about this project. Then we all toasted to the success of Families of America. I drank one more glass, but Mr. Henderson wouldn't stop drinking. His tongue was getting a little loose after three drinks. He came straight out and talked about how Mr. Ellis hired prostitutes for a congress party last year. That's when I knew it was time to go.

April rolled in and I kept asking Mr. Henderson when the construction could start. He told me by the end of April. When the end of April came, it was reported all over the news and newspapers that the city manager of housing development, Mr. Henderson, had a fatal accident. He was a heavy drinker and was a known functioning alcoholic. On his way home from a bar, he fell over the Martin Luther King Bridge. Word out that there was foul play involved. I heard it on the news and immediately called Mr. Ellis' office. His secretary told me he wasn't in, so I decided to try and see him personally. It was a little before 11:00 a.m. when I caught Mr. Ellis coming to his office on the last Tuesday of the month.

"Come on in, Mr. Harris," he said, leading the way.

I got straight to the point and said, "Mr. Ellis, were you there with Mr. Henderson at the bar?"

"James, you can call me Kevin. And for the record, I heard about it from one of my officials who called me early Monday morning."

"I hope this doesn't affect the project."

"I'm afraid so," Mr. Ellis said, pacing the floor and not looking me directly in the face. "It appears that Mr. Henderson had a fraudulent deed. I can get the papers for you by the morning."

"What!"

"I'm shocked just like you, but that's the word."

I didn't know what to do, so I said, "I'll have my lawyer contact you," and stormed out the office.

I got in contact with my lawyer and told him what happened. The next day, we got in contract with Mr. Ellis and the City Hall officials. We both went to the City Hall and got the whole scam told to us. It was an Ersatz land deal. Mr. Henderson was to blame for a lot of money that was missing from the government grant called TIFF.

Kevin Ellis tried to act as if he sincerely wanted to help by saying, "Listen, James. I know you already started the FA program, but there is not enough money to go ahead with the project. Why don't you let me buy your company, and I'll make some type of program where more jobs can be created in the urban community."

I couldn't believe what I was hearing, and as I looked at my lawyer, I could tell he could sense what I felt.

"We'll get back to you," I said, looking at my lawyer who was also ready to leave.

Mr. Ellis shook our hands and said, "I'm sorry things couldn't have worked out as planned."

As we boarded the elevator, I could tell my lawyer had the same impression I did. Mr. Ellis wanted to control all the government grants in the urban community. He wasn't even trying to hide it by showing any finesse. He was putting down a straight gangsta move. It took me a week to decide that I was going to take that million-dollar loss. I was ready to play another game though.

Chapter 12

Plan B

*There is no height to which we cannot climb by
using the active intelligence of our minds.*

—Marcus Garvey

I was out a million dollars. Let's not forget the fifty thousand my cousin never paid back, and the 1.5 million dollars that was stolen off a bus right from under me. I started looking at my portfolio and bank accounts. I decided to take my last quarter of a million out of the bank and invest it in something that would give me fast return.

It was in the middle of May when I brought my friends—T. I., Fats, and Li'l Darryl—over to my house. These guys were the only ones I could trust. They sat in the living room with the sound system blasting Tupac's CD. I made them turn it down when I came in the room because I was talking on the phone.

After I hung up, I said, "That was my lawyer. He was tellin' me that it's obvious that foul play was involved with Mr. Henderson's death, but it can't be proved. I know for a fact that Kevin Ellis is stealing funds from the TIFF program, but he's using Mr. Henderson's name as a scapegoat."

"I kinda figured that thurr. Dead men can't tell no tales," Fats said.

"You ain't figured a damn thing. You ain't no psychic," T. I. said, getting Li'l Darryl to laugh.

"Fuck you. And what you laughing at, ya' microwave-shaped head muthafucka?" Fats said to Li'l Darryl said.

I had to laugh at that one myself because Fats did have a big round bald head.

"Come on y'all. Let's get fa' real. I want us to make some major money."

"What you got in mind?" Fats asked.

"Do y'all have a drug connect?"

"Fa' sure," Fats said, looking at the others.

"Well, I want to know how much he'll change us for ten to twelve birds."

"About fifteen a piece," Fats said.

"Aiight, here's the plan. I'm fit'na give y'all a 150 grand. I want y'all to do the do. I don't want to know nothing. Just flip the drugs and we'll split the money."

They all looked serious while thinking.

Then T. I. said, "I'm wit'cha till the end."

"Me too," Fats said.

"You kno' I'mma ride," Li'l Darryl said.

The following months were very profitable. By the end of June, I had close to a half-million dollars back. I signed my name on cars for my boys. They were now all driving foreign cars.

I felt like an original hustler because back in the day, a hustler was seen as a hero who was against corrupt cops and the whole crooked system of law and justice. And a hustler would support his community.

I decided to get a contract with the construction company that was going to build the homes for my FA project and let them hire a few brothers in the hood who needed money. Of course, some of these brothers were working off the books because they were convicted felons that were on the run.

On the Fourth of July, the boys and I decided to get together in Lincoln Park and throw a barbecue. We went and got the best DJ in East St. Louis named DJ Dennis to spin the turntables. We had the grills out barbecuing steaks, burgers, and hot dogs. We had beers for the adults and sodas for the nondrinkers and children. Fats, T. I., Li'l Darryl, and hosts of others were kicking it while I cooked on the grill. Every girl in East St. Louis came through the park. One of my old flames, Jody, came through and we talked for a while. When she saw Corry and Torry coming with their friends, she left. That's when I let Ro take over the culinary skills the rest of the day, so I could be with Corry.

"Whassup, James," Torry said, hitting me with a fist on my shoulder.

"I see y'all are up to your old tricks by dressin' alike," I said.

"We don't want everybody to know the difference," Torry said.

"As long as y'all can't fool me," I said smiling.

"Nah. We already kno' that," Corry said.

After Torry went with the other girls, Corry and I started talking about where I've been. I told her the short version of everything that happened. Everybody knew that East St. Louis' officials and politicians were crooked. I knew that Judy had went back to Puerto Rico last month and wasn't due back for a week, so we left the park and went to my house before it go dark.

Soon as we got in my house, I said, "Make yourself at home. My house is your house. I'll be right back." And I went to the bathroom.

When I came out, Corry had to use the bathroom too. While I waited, I put my cell phone on vibrate and turned the stereo on.

Corry came out the bathroom smiling. "I'm not staying the night so don't—"

"I didn't ask you to," I said, smiling back.

We both sat on the sofa listening to Faith Evans and talking. She asked me about Judy, and I told her she still came to the house. I let her know there wasn't anything going on between us and hadn't for a while. Then I moved in on her space and kissed her. Next thing I knew, we were undressing and leaving a trail of clothes up to the bedroom. When I entered Corry, she felt as if she had an orgasm already. She was hot and wet. She wrapped her legs around my waist and rode me into orgasm after orgasm. After the second one, I rolled to the side, and she put her head on my chest and started kissing it.

"You still want me to take you home?"

"No. I'm staying her wit'chu."

"You know I want to be with you, Corry. I love you."

"I believe you," she said softly. "But if I love you back, I'll get hurt."

"How you figure that?"

"'Cause…you won't be faithful to me, and I can't stand that, James," Corry said, lifting her head up, looking me into the eyes.

I started rubbing her hair and said, "I won't hurt you if you come live with me."

"What about Jody?'

"Jody! What about her?" I said. "Jody was a redbone who lived in East St. Louis. We had messed with each other ever since I came back. No strings were attached."

"You still seeing her? I saw y'all in the park today."

"No. I'm not. Listen, we're just friends."

"Yeah. I heard that before. Friends end up as lovers."

"What I meant to say is that it's over. We left each other alone on good terms."

Corry just laid her head on my chest without saying anything. Then I felt the moistness on my chest and knew she was crying.

*****

When training camp started, I felt good. Money was flowing, and I had gained ten pounds over the summer. Narv Turner, the assistant coach, was on me about gaining more weight last season. We had acquired Lawrence Phillips, but it was controversy with him from day one. He stayed in trouble and was on the news. I got close to a few players and started taking them to the Platinum and Pink strip clubs. The players felt comfortable with me in the Pink Slip. It was raunchy, but the girls would play if you pay. There was never a dull day when I stepped in there. BYOBB (bring your own body bag) was my only motto to all the players. Some women were trifling enough to put holes in their condoms. Then there would be financial stability if they got pregnant by an athlete in their minds.

Once again, we started the season off bad. So when we were at home, we partied. I even took a few players to the Max to gamble. Then some of them tried going by themselves. Of course, they were cheated out of their money or stuck up in the parking lot.

In October, the coach got wind of the players going to the Pink Slip. He made an announcement at the practice, telling us to stop going over to Brooklyn because we're getting a bad reputation as a team.

On Thanksgiving, I was on my way back home when I saw Ron driving Jessica. We were on Broadway, and he pulled over to the side. I pulled over, and he got out first and made his way over to the car.

"Whassup, James. I've been try'na get up wit'chu for a while," Ron said.

"Yeah. Whassup."

"You member that restaurant in Belleville, right? Well, they 'bout to close. The reason I'm telling you is that's fa' sure money. We can go in it together," Ron said, putting his hands in his pockets because it was cold outside.

"Listen. You got my cell phone number still?"

"Yeah. But you don't answer it…"

"Call me Monday morning. Before nine o'clock."

"Aiight. I'll do that fa' sure," he said, running back to his Ford pickup.

When Monday came, Ron called like he said and ran the whole deal down to me about the restaurant. We went and checked it out, and I liked what I saw. It had enough room to do something with it. The price was not a problem. I knew that I could make my money back and some in a few years.

In December, I decided to buy the restaurant and let Ron run it for me. He came to me with less than ten thousand dollars and wanted to be a partner with me. It didn't matter. I could hold it down financially. I just needed someone to be there daily. I used the same construction company to upgrade the restaurant. It was ready for its grand opening in late March. I named it Legends. It was a sports bar and restaurant with sports pictures on the wall. It was real sophisticated. I had remembered my boy's restaurant in Puerto Rico. They had everything in order. I decided to do the same thing.

I had some of the players from the team to come down for the opening. By 5:00 p.m., I had an A-list-only crowd in the place. Ron had Jessica by his side wherever he went; she was wearing a cut-out back dress that hugged every curve on her body. The men were staring at Jessica's hoetry-in-motion walk, and Ron knew it. About that same time, Fats and T. I. came by on the motorcycles they just bought. That's when I brought out the case of Rothschild's Blanc Champagne and the red velvet double layer cake and got wasted. Take it from me that champagne and whisky don't mix. I couldn't even remember how I got home.

The year '97 was looking to be fruitful for me. With the restaurant running smoothly and my boys taking care of business on the streets, I had it going on. My bank account was back in order too. I even managed to start dating one of the tellers of my bank. Her name was Madonna. She was a White blond who lived in South County in Missouri. Well, she still lived with her parents in a big house. I would creep over to her place when Judy came to the house and I didn't want to be bothered. I would be intoxicated most of the time. Alcohol was part of my four basic food groups.

I was getting kind of hard to be around too. Don't get it twisted; I still had my boys' backs. I had my man Spaz who was part of my posse. He went everywhere with me. Like Cancun to see Puff Daddy and even to the strip clubs in the ATL. I also bought him a used Toyota 4-Runner and helped him purchase a house for his mother. For a friend, I would never turn my back on them.

In June, I told the whole posse to see the Evander Holyfield and Mike Tyson fight in Las Vegas. Fred the cop even came along. We couldn't get ringside seats because they were sold out in April right after the Pernall Whitaker versus Oscar De La Hoya. Fats, T. I., Spaz, and I went to that fight too. We were regulars in Sin City.

When we got back to East St. Louis; it was Sunday. I slept all day to recuperate. When Monday morning came, the doorbell was ringing. I went to the door and saw some plain-clothes White men with windbreakers on. My instinct told me they were FBI.

I opened the door and said, "May I help you?"

"Mr. James Harris," a six-foot-tall blond-haired agent said. "You're under arrest."

He started to read me my rights, but I wasn't paying attention. I needed to get my lawyer and wasn't talking to anyone until I saw him.

Chapter 13

Public Enemy #1

Of all the disorders of the soul, envy is the only one no one confesses to.

—Plutarch

After playing the good cop, bad cop, they let me put on some clothes and escorted me to a beige Marquis. I was then driven downtown to the federal building in East St. Louis on Missouri Street. I was given a phone call to contact my lawyer and then put in a holding cell. The good cop, who was a DEA agent, came and told me my wife said she would be down to see me. I had just missed her when they took me out of the house.

My lawyer finally came in looking frantic and said, "I heard the charges are for conspiracy. I'm going to get you a bond, but they are looking for your conspirators."

"I don' know what's going on yet," I said, frustrated.

I went in front of a magistrate judge and bail was set at thirty-seven million dollars. That meant I would have to stay in jail until my bond was dropped.

Before I was taken off to the federal holding facility, my lawyer came to see me and said, "Your next bond hearing, I will arrange for you to get a reduced bond."

"I'll call you tomorrow morning," I said.

"I hope so. Another thing is I'll have to assign you to another lawyer. Fredrick Hess of Lewis, Rice, and Fengurhist is the best firm I know of in the state. I'll let you know you're a client of mine."

"Thanks a lot," I said.

I was taken to jail and would have to wait patiently. I wasn't in the mood for any socializing, so I stayed in my cell and slept most of the day until the morning. I didn't feel like eating, but I ate some cereal. Then I asked a Black female CO if I could use the phone. She was more than happy to help me. The first person I called was my man Spaz. I heard the phone pick up on the second ring.

Then his voice came in after the collect call recorder, and he said, "Whassup, kinfolk. I heard what went down."

"Yeah, man. They got me fucked up. I ain't do shit."

"I know that's right. What you need me to do?"

"Call Ron at the restaurant and tell him to get up wit' T. I. and tell him to contact my lawyer," I said, running the phone number down to him.

"I'm fid'na do it right now," Spaz said.

I called my lawyer a little later, and he told me I would get another bail hearing on Thursday. When Thursday came, they agreed to let me go if I put my house and one million dollars. My new attorney had a good repute with the judge. I was out before lunch.

I had to take a cab from East St. Louis to my house in West County. I opened the door and saw a trail of clothes coming down the stairs. I went up to the bedroom and all Judy's clothes were gone. I went to check my stash spot in the bedroom, and sure enough, a hundred thousand dollars was gone. The bitch robbed me. I knew it was her and not the Feds because her clothes were gone. I called Fats immediately.

He picked up on the first ring and said, "What's up?"

"I hope you're in a safe spot."

"I should be askin' you that. It's all on the news."

"Listen, man. It'll be aiight. Just turn ya'self in and—"

"What! Man…I don't kno' bout dat thurr."

"Listen, kinfolk. I'm on ya' side. I'll put up some money to get ya' out. I got ya' back."

"Give me a couple of days to take care of some business," Fats said.

"Aiight. I'll holla at ya' later," I said, hanging up.

Four days later on a Monday morning, Fats, T. I., Li'l Darryl, and thirty-three others were picked up. I got Fats, T. I., and Li'l Darryl out in a few days.

The media made a big hoopla about the case by reporting that I was the alleged money supplier in a big cocaine ring outside East St. Louis. I went to see my lawyer in downtown St. Louis on Thursday morning. I stepped in the firm office of Lewis, Rice, and Fengurhist at 9:30 a.m. and saw a professionally dressed Black woman walk by with files in her hand.

"Good morning," I said smiling.

"Good morning," she said, stopping. "Can I help you?"

"I'm here to see Atty. Hess."

"You must be Mr. Harris," she said, looking at me from head to toe.

"Yes, that's me."

"He's running a little late, but you can have a seat."

"Thank you," I said, sitting down.

She went in an office and came right back out with her hands empty and said, "I've never seen you here before."

"Well, this is my first time. My lawyer referred me to come here. Told me these were the best attorneys in all of St. Louis."

"I hear that a lot too. You're the football player that's in *Jet Magazine*."

"I am?"

"Yeah. Haven't you seen it?"

"I'm afraid I haven't," I said as she went in an office and reappeared with the issue of *Jet Magazine*.

"Here you go," she said, handing it to me.

I sat and read the article on me. Just as I was almost finished, Mr. Hess came through the door. He was dressed in the typical Brooks Brother suit and toting a lambskin briefcase.

"Good morning, Ms. Brooks and Mr. Harris. I'm sorry I'm so late. Got caught up in traffic."

"That's all right," I said, trying to let him know it meant nothing.
"Come in the office so we can talk," he said.

I went in his office, and we got straight down to work. Mr. Hess was in his early forties but looked older. He was definitely a workaholic. I felt comfortable with him and told him that I was implemented into a drug conspiracy charge, and that's all I knew. He assured me that he would get all the information he could and that I must tell him everything I know because he was working for me. I left out an hour later feeling confident in letting him represent me. He told me he would do the arguing, and Ron Norway would do the research.

The following week, I was in the *Sports Illustrated* magazine. That's when I got a call from some of the players on my team and around the league wishing me the best and giving me support. Then finally, Coach Vermeil called and asked me what happened. I told him I was innocent, and it would be proven so.

The whole summer was stressful for me. I couldn't help but think about my case. On the Fourth of July, Fats, T. I., Li'l Darryl, and I were barbecuing out at Fats' house.

And the Feds came driving by and said, "Gentlemen. Enjoy one of the holidays in the real world," and then drove off laughing.

"Fuck them!" Fats said.

"Yeah. We need to have fun till it's time to do our time," T. I. said.

"Yeah. We've got a few months to go," I said.

"Man, I ain't try'na be thinkin' 'bout that every day. Let's go out to Chicago on our bikes," Li'l Darryl said.

And that's how we did it. We went everywhere in the month of July. When I reported to spring training, all the coaches were asking me questions about the case. The main one was if I was selling drugs. I was finally called up after practice during preseason to see the owner.

All the coaches were not present when I entered the office. There were a few faces I'd never seen before. They were all seated facing me while I stood up. The owner started asking questions about if I like playing football. Then he asked me about the case and if I was guilty.

Of course, I said I was not. He nodded his head and proceeded to ask a few questions. It was as if he was trying to find out what my chances were winning the case. Dick Vermeil finally spoke up for me by stating that I was a good kid and stayed out of trouble. The owner was looking at me while Coach Vermeil was speaking.

After the coach finished, the owner said, "I'm willing to support you, Mr. Harris. You're innocent until proven guilty. We'll let justice prevail. Just remember that you're in the public's eyes of scrutiny. Don't talk about your case to anyone."

I agreed to everything they said and left the office.

The following weekend, we had a preseason game. We were on the field scrimmaging against the Colts at the University of Illinois when everybody saw Fats, T. I., and Li'l Darryl pull up in 928 Porsche to come watch me play. They had diamonds on their fingers and rocks in their ears. The coaches watched them cheering me on and hollering my name. Of course, I acknowledged them. The coaches already knew they were my posse.

Immediately after the game, the coaches told me I needed to stop hanging with my boys and start working harder on conditioning my body. So I went inside the facility to hit some weights with a few of the players. Orland Pace had just joined the team, so a lot of the offensive and defensive linemen were competing to see who was the strongest. I didn't like to work out with the barbell. I just liked to use dumbbells. While I was doing my chest routine, a few of the players were trying to get me to do the barbell.

One of the players finally said, "That's why you're going to lose your spot."

I finished my final set of reps, which was some 110-pound dumbbells, and said, "I make more money on the streets than you do for the Rams," and walked out of the weight room.

The following week, I attended church with my grandmother, and to my surprise, Coach Vermeil came along too. He came to my grandmother's house, and I rode with him to the church. I was surprised he wanted to be around me.

When we got there, the service was about to begin. We found a spot while the choir was singing. All eyes were on us.

Rev. Woods opened by talking about having faith. Then he gave a speech on the Book of Job. He said, "Job feared God and had everything he needed because he was perfect and upright man. But he was put to the test by losing everything he had. He still feared God and held his tongue from blaspheming him. Job asked God to give him understanding. He stayed patient and complained in the bitterness of his soul. His will to live was strong, but he complained in prayer to God. Satan tried to convince Job to his wicked ways so that he could prosper with worldly possessions at the present time, but Job refused. He had confidence in God's mercy."

I listened as Rev. Woods gave a great sermon. It sounded as if he was talking to me. I sold my soul to the devil and didn't have to. God blessed me with the talent to play football and to think for myself.

After the sermon, Coach Vermeil and I stayed, and my grandmother introduced the coach to Rev. Woods. We all took pictures together. Then the reverend put in a good word for me about having a good family and being a God-fearing individual as long as he could remember. Coach Vermeil looked as if he was amused when he left the church and went home.

It was September 1, 1997, when I went to start picking my jury. They had separated all of us in the case, so I was going to trial by myself. Judge Reilly was the judge for my case. Mr. Hess and Mr. Norway, my attorneys, were as prepared as they could be. I had two private investigators working my case too. We stayed in court the whole Monday morning, picking the jury. My attorney tried to pick them as young as he possibly could. He only picked women; he knew men liked to watch football and would remember the image of me as a football player. We went through fifty-five people before we were satisfied.

After jury selection, we went back to the office to go over my PSI report and witness list. Ms. Brooks was still in the office eating Chinese food with the secretary.

"Good afternoon, Freddy and Mr. Harris," Ms. Brooks said.

We both spoke to her and went in his office.

"Mr. Harris, I want you to be honest with me, which I feel you have been so far. But…I've found out two witnesses in your case that are going to testify against you. They are Maurice Finley and Jeffrey Hall."

I thought about the names he said and only knew Maurice Finley. That was Keisha and Teisha's father.

"I'm familiar with Maurice Finley. I look after his two daughters from time to time."

"Good. We have little more to go on him," Mr. Lewis said.

We looked over my PSI report and just agreed to focus on the two witnesses. I left the office a little after 2:00 p.m. and drove to my grandmother's house. I was glad to see she was home watching he soap operas.

"You might as well sit down wit' me. I need to talk to you," she said, turning the television volume down.

I sat down next to her on the sofa and said, "What's on ya' mind, Grandma?"

"You on my mind, son. I've been worrying 'bout ya'."

"You don't have ta worry 'bout me."

"Yes, I do. Them so-called friends of yours done got you in trouble. They all jealous of ya'. You need to leave every one of them alone," she said as my cell phone started ringing.

I answered it and it was Corry. I told her that I would stop by her house before I went home.

"I don't wanna preach to ya'. It's too late for that, but you're the cream of the crop of East St. Louis. Don't let nobody bring you down. Promise me you'll read Psalms 17?"

"I promise," I said, nodding my head.

Before I left, I ate some barbecued chicken and collard greens she made and fixed the color on her television. Then I left four hundred dollars under her pillow.

I drove over to check on Corry, and Torry answered the door before I rang the bell.

"You might as well come in and sit down," she said, grabbing me by the arm.

Corry was coming down the stairs in her work clothes as I sat down. She came over to kiss and hug me before I could say anything.

"You forgot all about me, huh?" she said.

"No," I said. "It's just been crazy the last month…"
"Well, let me tell you what I heard at work," Torry said.
"Speaking of work, I gotta go," Corry said.
"I'll call you tonight," I told her.
"I'm going to hold your word to that," Corry said, leaving out the door.
"Now what're you talking about?"
"You're fuckin' friend, Spaz. His mom was on the boat drunk and talkin' shit about you. She made it seem like you ain't shit, and her son is God's gift to East St. Louis."
"What did you hear her saying?"
"She said you called her son and expected him to come bail you out of jail."
"What! He can't even pay my lawyer's fee."
"I know that's right," Torry said, telling me more and more of what everyone was saying around town.

I told her about Maurice being a witness against me. I told her to not tell Corry. I wanted to tell her myself, then I asked her if she know Jeffrey Hall.

"Yah, I know his ass. He's a crackhead. Be on 18th Street all the time."

We talked until it was dark outside. Then I drove straight home thinking about Spaz. He didn't even make the calls for me on the day I was in jail. Now I know why. He really didn't care for me. As I drove home, my soul felt like it had been punctured by my friends. I knew Ron was skimming money from the restaurant books. And Maurice wanting to testify in court against me was really hurting. They were all poking an ice pick in my heart and through my kindness. I was bleeding and losing energy.

I made it home and went straight to the jacuzzi with a bottle of Jack Daniels. When I got out of the water, I dried off and felt like looking at the television. I turned it on Sports Center when I got to my bedroom and saw myself on the screen. The St. Louis Rams had cut me.

Chapter 14

Judgment Day

*The man or woman who has no confidence
in self is an unfortunate being.*

—Marcus Garvey

Missouri's street was filled with reporters and cameras from the St. Louis Dispatch and other publications. October 23, 1997, was the day that would change my life; that was what I was thinking as I got out of the limousine with my two attorneys. We went straight in the Federal Building without talking to anybody. The elevator was waiting for us as we entered and went straight to the third floor. My attorneys asked the judge for my case to be sealed because of my profession, but it was denied. My case was open for any and everybody to hear about or see. It was even on the Internet.

It was a full house inside the courtroom. My attorneys told me that the St. Louis Rams had legal experts in the room too. They were the ones that told the organization that I would be found guilty. That's why I was cut. Mr. Hess had a lot of confidence that I would walk out the courthouse an innocent man. I had confidence I would walk too. I'd read Psalms 17 before coming to court and knew that God would pave the way.

With Fats testifying that I had nothing to do with 150-kilo conspiracy, I had faith. The only thing that had me a little shaken was the US attorney, Patrick Skiles, whose nickname was Pitbull because he would lock down on a case and wouldn't let go until he got a conviction. He had wanted to talk to me about Jeffrey Hall being murdered. My attorney told him that I had nothing to say about the murder to him unless I was being charged for it.

I spotted my mother and Uncle Junebug. They were seated directly behind me and my friends and people who I'd seen around East St. Louis. I nodded and waved at my mother and uncle. Then I saw the US attorney enter the courtroom and knew the judge would be coming soon. When Judge Reilly entered the courtroom and nine o'clock sharp, everybody rose until he sat and the bailiff yelled, "Please be seated!"

Judge Reilly cleared his throat and went through the procedure of stating the docket number and United States of America versus James Harris, which made my heart beat a little faster. Then he looked up after shuffling the papers in front of him and said, "Are we ready to proceed?"

"Yes, Your Honor," said Mr. Skiles.

"Good. And you, Mr. Hess?"

"Yes, Your Honor," said my attorney.

"Good. Then you can go first," said Judge Reilly looking at Mr. Hess.

"Yes, Your Honor. Concerning the amount of media exposure on the case, I'm going to stick to concrete evidence as much as possible."

"This is a conspiracy case, correct?"

"Yes, Your Honor. But there has to be a line drawn to what is admissible and what is hearsay."

"I understand what you are saying. Proceed."

My attorney turned to the US attorney and gave him the floor. Mr. Skiles immediately mentioned my lifestyle and how I flaunted it. He was painting a vivid picture of me being an athlete that was a ghetto superstar in my hood. A professional athlete but a modern-day Robin Hood. The Pitbull in hiding came out fast.

Now he was ready for his first witness. "I want to call Maurice Finley to the stand."

Maurice came from out the back wearing Polo Jeans and a button-up Polo shirt and was quickly sworn in.

Then the Pitbull got down to business. "Mr. Finley, do you or do you not have charges pending against you including the possession and sale of cocaine?"

"Yes, sir."

"Do you recall entering a guilty plea and having a plea agreement with the United States Government?"

"Yes, sir."

"Do you know the defendant right over there?" asked Mr. Skiles, pointing in my direction.

"Yes, sir."

"Do you know him by any particular name?"

"James Harris."

"Let me draw your attention back to the summer of '96 up to the spring of '97. Would you tell the court in your own words what you were doing during that period and how you knew the defendant?"

Maurice went into a spill that he was selling drugs on 18th and Broadway for Fats and that everybody new Fats was my main. Fats had an unlimited supply of cocaine and had to be getting the money from me to supply East St. Louis. It was all he kept saying at the end of every answer.

When it was time for cross-examination, Mr. Hess paced the floor real slow and got right up in Maurice's face and said, "Mr. Finley, through your whole testimony, not once did I hear you say that Mr. Hawkins told you himself that he got money for drugs for Mr. Harris."

"He didn't. But like I said, they were best friends."

"Is that right? Could you explain this to the courtroom," Mr. Hess said, folding his arm across his chest.

"He's a millionaire. A made man. He'll do anything for his friends."

"Is it true Mr. Harris looks after your daughters occasionally and takes them to his house?"

"I'm not aware of that," Maurice said.

"Your Honor, I would like his testimony to be found inadmissible…"

"I object, sir. His testimony is based on the fact that he grew up with these fellas and worked for one of them," Mr. Skiles said.

"I'd like to all Mr. Damon Hawkins to the stand," said Mr. Hess.

Maurice was escorted away, and Fats was brought out. He was sworn in and he stated his name. He went through the procedure of pointing me out for the courts. He stated that he was sentenced to fifteen months and that I never gave him money for drugs. The only thing I did was help him buy a Porsche and a motorcycle. He then stated that he had a garage, and he raced bikes and cars for a living.

Mr. Skiles was antsy in his seat listening to Fats' testimony. When it was his turn, he said, "Where did you get the money for the garage?"

"From my family. That garage was passed down to me from my uncle."

"Is it true that you were implemented in the murder of the key witness, Jeffrey Hall, on this case?"

"Objection, Your Honor."

"Sustained. Mr. Skiles, you must stay in the scope of the case."

"Your Honor. My key witness was murdered, and he could have sealed this case shut. Don't you think the jury has the right to know if Mr. Hawkins had something to do with it?"

"Proceed, Mr. Skiles."

Pitbull was pulling out all the punches but couldn't get the response he wanted.

He looked at Farts and said, "Were you not the first suspect to be brought in when Jeffrey Hall was murdered?"

"Yes but—"

"No further comment. You were implemented in the murder because Jeffrey Hall was a key witness against you and Mr. Harris."

"Yeah, but—"

"If there was a witness that saw him get shot, I'm sure the murder would lead back to you and Mr. Harris hiring the killer."

"Objection, Your Honor! He's putting thoughts in the jury's mind. My client is a well-respected citizen who is on trial for conspiracy of drugs, not murder."

Judge Reilly made the Pitbull tone it down, but the jury heard what they needed to hear.

Mr. Hess wanted to ask Fats more questions but didn't want to seem as if he was desperate to get his point across, so he left Fats alone.

I went on the stand next and talked about the Porsches I bought Fats, T. I., and Li'l Darryl for the car racing they did mostly in Joliet, Illinois. I even explained to the courtroom that they had a harness in each car for racing protection. Then I told them how I took care of Maurice's daughters and about the restaurant I had. Mr. Hess made sure that he asked me about my relationship with Maurice. My reply was that I never spoke to him under any circumstances in the last two years.

Mr. Skiles couldn't cross-examine me the way he wanted to. All he could bring up was the murder of Jeffrey Hall. I told the courtroom that I didn't even know who Jeffrey Hall was. They jury looked as if they were undecided, but I wasn't a mind reader.

When Mr. Skiles didn't have any other witnesses, my other attorney, Mr. Norway, took over by putting people from the community who were all respected on the stand. Mrs. Shavers and Rev. Woods were the most effective. They said they never saw me around the drug zone areas involved in anything negative. Judy Reilly then asked me about the Families of America Program he heard about. This got the Pitbull riled up. He called Kenny Thomas to the stand when I was seated. I knew Ken. He was part of the big indictment and was already sentenced. He came out and was sworn in. My attorney, Mr. Hess, said something to the judge about last-minute witnesses needed to be declared to the defense, which was ignored.

Mr. Skiles proceeded and said, "State what you were doing in the summer of '96 up until the spring of '97."

"I was in the East St. Louis. I was working and got caught selling drugs."

"Who were you selling for?"

"Well, you'll want me to say Fats, but I stole for myself or anybody that had work."

There was a lot of whispering going through the courtroom. My attorneys looked at each other and started smiling.

Mr. Skiles paced the floor between the jury and Ken and then walked over to him and said, "Have you ever seen Mr. Harris before?"

"Yeah. But not doing nothing illegal," Ken said with a serious face.

Mr. Skiles was turning beet red. He had nothing else to say to Ken, so he went into the rhetoric about Ken selling drugs, and out of nowhere, he said that I was polygamist. He brought up Judy Krude's name and Bonnie's name as the two I was married to at the same time and then sat down, leaving the jury in a buzz.

Mr. Hess excused Ken off the stand and then my other attorney, Mr. Norway, showed the courtroom the papers to prove that I was married to Bonnie and that Judy was just girlfriend who lived with me around a year or so. She had some false marriage papers made up to impress her parents back in Puerto Rico because they did not believe in her living with a man unless she was married to him. Then the false marriage papers were passed around jury.

The last statements were made first by my attorney and the US attorney. I felt firsthand why they called him Pitbull because he wouldn't give up. He brought up that Minnesota Vikings had heard rumors that I was selling drugs in Minneapolis and St. Paul.

The verdict came in after lunch at approximately 2:15 p.m., and I was found not guilty. I stood up and loosened my tie to my tailor-made suit and exhaled a sigh of relief. I had been holding my breath waiting to hear the verdict. I hugged my family and friends and then made my way outside to the limo with my attorneys right behind me.

Chapter 15

Hate Me Now

To be paranoid is to be very aware.

—Charles Manson

When we made it back to the attorney's office, to my surprise, Ms. Brooks was there.

"Yeah. We did it again. I won another big case," Mr. Hess said, sounding arrogant and excluding Mr. Norway.

"I knew you would. And how do you feel, Mr. Harris?" Ms. Brooks said.

"I feel relieved," I said. "Thanks for being concerned."

"I couldn't help it," she said, getting up and walking across the room in her Patton leather pumps and navy-blue skirt suit. She went in her office but left the door wide open.

I took that as an invitation and walked over by her door. "Are you busy this weekend?" I asked her while standing in the doorway with my hands in my pockets.

"Uh…no," she said, looking up at me from shuffling paper on her desk.

"Good. I want to take you to see my restaurant."

"I would like to do that, but I wanna know one thing."

"What?" I said with a smile on my face.

"Is this a date?"

"Yeah. You could say that."

"Then I can stop calling you Mr. Harris, right?"

"Of course. Call me James. And…"

"Shavonne," she said with a smile on her face.

We talked a little more before I left but not before thanking Mr. Hess and Mr. Norway once again.

When I got home, I got a call from everybody. My agent, Ron, and Spaz were the main calls. My agent said he would look for a team to pick me up as soon as possible. I told Ron that I wanted to expand the restaurant by using some of the space in the parking lot to build a dance floor and an indoor swimming pool. I wanted to make it more of a sports club than a restaurant. I knew it would be even more successful.

The following day, I went to East St. Louis to see my mother and brother. When I pulled up in front of the house, a cop car pulled up behind me. I looked before getting out and saw it was Fred.

"Hey, James. I'm glad to see that you came out all right. You're a good dude. Stay away from these losers around here."

"I know that's right," I said, looking at my watch, trying to give him a hint that I was pressed for time.

"I just wanted to holla at ya' real quick like," Fred said, walking back to the car.

"Aiight now. We'll kick it later," I said.

When I went in the house, my mother, brother, Uncle Junebug were all in the living room. My uncle was still looking out the window when I closed the door.

"What did that snake have to say to ya'?" my uncle said.

"Jus' that I need to leave tha dudes 'lone 'round here."

"He right about that. He needs to include himself," my mother said. "It's not easy to be found not guilty in a federal court."

"Ya' mother tellin' ya' right. I see a lot of things, but you're the first person I kno' that beat the Feds," Uncle Junebug said, sitting down on the sofa next to my brother.

I looked at my uncle and then back at my brother. They looked just alike.

My brother was pulling out a hangnail on his index finger as Uncle Junebug went on and said, "Those friends you got ain't really your friends. As soon as you stop giving them things, they'll stop comin' 'round you."

I took in everything my uncle said because he knew what he was talking about. The more I thought about my relationships with my friends, the more I realized that I wasn't really helping them because I wasn't letting them be men and make their own way. In reality, they hated me for what I was doing for them. But in the same token, I didn't want it to look like I'd turned my back on my hood because I was making big money. I'm from East Boogie and will never forget where I came from.

The following weeks were all about Shavonne. I took her to my restaurant and then went shopping down the Magnificent Mile in Chicago. Then we went over 89th Street to Harold's Chicken. Shavonne was a little uncomfortable when she saw how the restaurant had bulletproof windows, but I assured her that this was the spot that had the best chicken in the Midwest. After tasting it, she agreed with me. The following week, we went back to Chicago and attended Ebony Fashion Fair Show. It was a week before Thanksgiving when Shavonne called me on Monday morning with the shocking news. I picked up the phone on the third ring and heard her voice.

"I'm surprised you calling me early."

"I'm at work and thought you might want to hear the news from me first."

"What are you talking about?"

"Judge Reilly...the judge on your case. Well, he has been indicted."

"What!"

"Yeah. Mr. Hess is going to call you as soon as he gets in. It came up on the fax machine in our office early this morning."

"Are you sure it's Judge Reilly?"

"Yes, James. It says here that they think he took a bribe in your case."

"I don't believe that."

"Believe it, James. I have to get some work done."

"Aiight. I'll talk to you later," I said, hanging up.

Later on that day, I called the office and got ahold of Mr. Hess. He explained to me that the Feds believed Judge Reilly took a bribe from him through me and that he was under investigation for doing this. If he is found guilty, they will reopen my case for another trial. This wasn't what I wanted to hear. If he is found guilty, I would have to go through the ordeal again, and I know I would be found guilty.

Thanksgiving came and I decided to spend it with my family and Shavonne's family. We had decided to go to my family's first and then her parents' house. I picked her up at her apartment on the west side of St. Louis. She was wearing a beautiful Chanel outfit she'd bought when we went shopping in Chicago. She got in the Lexus, and I could see that she went to the beauty parlor too.

"Hmmm, you look like you're ready to go out on a date."

"First impression…I wanna look decent when I meet your family."

"Don't worry about your looks. Just be yourself," I said as I drove off.

We got to my grandmother's house, and it wasn't even noon, but I could tell everybody had started drinking. When we walked in, Uncle Junebug, my grandmother, and some distant cousins were all in the living room shouting over Earth, Wind, and Fire's "Shining Star" that was playing on my grandmother's old stereo. She had all the eight tracks out on the floor going through them.

When she looked up and saw me, she said, "Boy, I didn't hear ya' come in."

"The music is playing loud," I said.

She stood up, and I walked over to her holding Shavonne's hand.

"Grandma, this is Shavonne."

"Nice to meet you. You're a lawyer, right?"

"Yes, ma'am."

"I've heard. Well, make yourself comfortable," my grandmother said as I introduced her to everybody in the room.

My brother and mother were in the kitchen, so I went in to see what they were doing. Of course, Shavonne was right behind me. I walked in the kitchen, and they had their backs to me taking sweet potato pies out of the oven. Well, my brother was actually cutting a piece out of one of them.

"Hey!" I said making them both turn around quickly.

"Whut up, bro," my brother said, never taking his eye off his piece of pie.

"I'm glad you got here early," my mother said.

"I want y'all to meet somebody," I said, introducing Shavonne to both of them.

My mother was talking to Shavonne as my brother was telling me that Cousin Earl was on his way.

"Man, I haven't seen him since last year. He kno' I'm over here?"

"I guess so. I don't know," Eric said, biting into his pie.

I went and cut me a piece and Mother said, "I knew you weren't going to wait."

When Earl came in the house, everybody was about to eat. Now my family is a little different when it comes to holiday meals; we don't sit at tables all at once. Everybody was scattered around the house. My grandmother, Shavonne, and my older female cousins were in the dining room eating, and the men were in the living room. Earl and I stayed in the kitchen to eat. He said he wanted to talk to me in private. So we talked in general about my trial and my boys.

Then he popped the big question on me. "I know I owe you some money."

"Some money? Fifty thousand is—"

"Jus' hear me out, cuz. I'm 'bout to get that and more, but I need your help. All I need is twenty thousand."

Now why did I even consider listening to him? I guess it's because he is family, and I have a kind heart.

"I kno' what you thinkin', but Imma get your money back to ya' before Christmas. My son needs some Christmas clothes, and I can hustle because everybody locked up. I fucked up before, but I promise you on everything I love, I gotcha this time."

By the time I finished eating, I decided to give Earl the money. I told him to stop by the restaurant tomorrow afternoon. I went to see how Shavonne was doing, and she was in the middle of speaking when I walked in the dining room. She looked quite comfortable, but I knew she was ready to go because I promised her we'd leave before two o'clock to go over to her parents' house.

We got back to St. Louis and pulled up in front of her parents' house in North County a little before three. She had told me that her mother was a social worker and her father an architect, but that was all I knew about them. She rang the doorbell, and her mother answered the door.

"Mrs. Brooks. It's nice to finally meet you," I said.

"Likewise. I've heard a lot about you," Shavonne's mother said before moving to the side to let us in.

There were other family members in the house, and I was introduced to aunts, uncles, and cousins. Mr. Brooks had heard about my legal problems on ESPN and made a statement that he was glad to hear that I was innocent on the charges. Then we gathered around the table to eat. I was sitting between Shavonne and one of her teenage cousins named Niecy. They all looked alike. Mrs. Brooks, Shavonne, and Niecy were all a butterscotch complexion with pretty light-brown eyes. Mr. Brooks said grace and we all ate. It was just like what you see on a television show minus the drama. We passed bowls of food around the table. Shavonne only ate al little because she ate at my grandmother's house, but I had room for more.

After everybody finished eating, Mr. Brooks took me down to the basement to shoot some pool with two of his brothers. That's when all the questions were thrown at me about my career. I could only tell them I wasn't playing at the moment. I could feel the room get a little cold after a while and knew it was time to leave, so I told them I had to use the bathroom and went upstairs.

Shavonne and I were only seeing each other for a few weeks, but we connected and could read each other's vibes. She took one look at me and knew something was wrong.

While her aunts were talking, she looked at her watch and said, "Are you ready to take me home? You know I got to go to work tomorrow."

"It's only six o'clock," Mrs. Brooks said.

"I kno', Ma, but James has to go home too."

"All right. When are you coming back by? You know you'll disappear for a month or two like you live in another state."

"Christmas is around the corner," Shavonne said, leaving the room.

I told all four women that it was nice meeting them. You could tell they were all sisters too. They could all not say a word but still be talking to each other. That was my family too. I was glad when Shavonne came back in the room with her coat. She hugged her aunts, and I just said good night as we left the house.

"Your father don't like me," I said as we were getting in the car.

"He don't like nobody."

"What about your mother?"

"What about her? As long as I like you, that's what counts," she said, getting in the car.

While I was driving Shavonne to her apartment, she said, "Let's go to your house."

I didn't even respond. I just changed my course and headed for West County.

I pulled up in the garage, and when we got out, she said, "Your house looks nice at night."

"Thanks," I said, walking toward the door.

We got inside and I told her that I'd be right back. I liked to walk around the entire house to make sure nobody else is in the house besides me. I went back to the living room, and Shavonne was looking at the movie collection.

"You go a lot of movies."

"Yeah. You want to look at one?"

"Yeah."

"Aiight, pick anyone you want. You want something to drink?"

"You got champagne?"

"I think I got one bottle," I said.

I went to the bar, and I grabbed a bottle of Rothschild Champagne. When I got back to the living room, she was still looking at my movie collection. I poured her a glass first and then myself. I gave it to her and watched her take a sip.

"Ooh. I know this not what I think it is," she said.

"Yes, it is," I said, thinking she was talking about *the* champagne.

She pulled out one of my X-rated tapes and said, "I always wanted to look at one of these before."

"I'll put it in," I said, taking it from her hand.

It was called *My Baby Got Back*. We sat on the sofa sipping champagne and watching the movie.

"Mmm, that man is too big for that girl's mouth," Shavonne said.

"These are professionals. Watch this," I said as the girl put it in her mouth and, after a while, had it down her throat.

Shavonne wasn't just looking at it, she was analyzing the scene. The next sex scene took her over the top. The couple was on the sofa, and the girl was on top of the man with her feet on his thighs, reverse cowgirl style.

"She's a contortionist," she said. "Could you turn the volume down? The noise is too much.

I put it on mute and just let the scene roll.

"I know you have a lot of women over here."

"No. I haven't seen anybody at all since I met you at the firm."

She sipped her champagne and said, "That was so corny that I know it is sincere." Then she kissed me.

That was all it took. We fell to the floor and undressed each other. Our tongues traveled each other's bodies as if we were some type of delicacy. When we finally had sex, it was an explosion when we came. Then we fell into a rhythm and had a marathon lovemaking session.

The next day, I was awakened by the phone at noon. It was Earl calling from the restaurant on his cell phone. I told him I would be there in no less than a half hour. I left Shavonne in bed and told her to make herself at home. When I got to the restaurant, Earl was at the bar eating Buffalo wings and drinking a Heineken out of a beer glass. I got the same thing he was eating and listened to him talk about what he was going to do with the money and how fast he could do it. I gave him the twenty thousand dollars just before I had finished eating. Then I went and told Ron that I was going to start rebuilding in a couple of weeks and left.

On my way back home, it seemed as though I was being followed by a Chevy SUV, but it turned off when I was back in St. Louis.

Shavonne and I stayed in the house the whole weekend. She had a lot of energy, and I loved every bit of it. We looked at my whole porno collection, and as I said before, she analyzed the movies and performed a lot of the movements she saw very well.

The following week, she went back to work, and we talked every day on the phone. Then she brought some of her clothes to my house the following week.

A week before Christmas, I was hit with shocking news. My lawyer called and told me that Judge Reilly died of a heart attack. The meant the indictment was closed on him. Then just before I left the house for the restaurant, my agent called and told me that the Oakland Raiders wanted to sign me, but I would have to pass the physical. All this news was good to me as I was driving to my restaurant.

When I pulled up in the parking lot, I noticed a forest-green Range Rover sticking an instrument out the window in my direction. When I got out of my vehicle, they drove off.

I went inside and Earl surprised me when he handed me some money and said, "Merry Christmas, cuz."

"How much is this?" I asked while putting it in my pocket.

"Thirty geez. Listen, cuz…I can make it happen fa' real. All I need is fa' ya' to hit me wit' anotha' twenty grand and…"

"Slow down, baby. What do you need? I'll get it fa' ya'."

"I need a brick," Earl said.

"How 'bout I get'cha two."

"That'll work."

"Aiight then. Come by on Saturday."

"Fa' sure, kinfolk. Later," he said, leaving the restaurant and jogging over to his Ford pickup.

The holiday season went by without me even noticing. I bought presents for everyone. Shavonne got me a Ferragamo shirt and tie. I got her an iced tennis bracelet. I was so involved with the restaurant that nothing else got my fully divided attention at the time. I wasn't checking no one at the time. I was busy changing the restaurant into a club. I went and got Ro to hook me up with one of Fats' connect and bought the cocaine myself and gave it to Earl.

It was February of '98 when I decided to buy Shavonne a nice present for Valentine's Day. I went and bought her a five-carat crystal-clear diamond ring for a quarter of a million. I pulled up in my black Lexus in front of her apartment, and she came outside right away looking good in a skirt and leather jacket with mink on the collar.

"Happy Valentine's Day," I said, kissing her on the lips.

"Mmm. I hope you plan to give me a better kiss than that."

"Let me do this," I said, driving off.

I drove out to the Westfield Northwest Shopping Town and found a favorite seafood restaurant. Shavonne ordered lobster and shrimp. I ordered bluefish and crab legs. We drank a little white wine and talked about my restaurant and how her firm didn't want to make her a partner. When she went to the restroom, I put the velvet box on the table in front of her spot. She came back to sit down and looked down at it.

"Open it. It's yours."

She looked at. Then picked it up and shook it.

"Open the damn box, woman."

"Wait!" she said.

When she opened it and saw what it was, her eyes instantly started getting watery. "James! No, you didn't!"

"Yes, I did. It's official. We're engaged."

"Put it on my finger," she said. "I'm not never taking it off ever."

I put it on then gave her kiss. When we got back to my house, we made love that was so passionate that we never made it to the bed. We fell asleep on the living room floor.

The following week, Shavonne moved in to live with me. It appeared that there was always a car or jeep passing by my house that whole week. The reason I noticed was because I didn't have any neighbors closer than a quarter of a mile.

By the summer, I was finished remodeling the restaurant. The last Friday of June, I opened the doors to the new and improved

Legends Restaurant, and it was packed. Jackie Joyner Kersee, Marshall Faulk, Isaac Bruce, and other celebrities and actors came through the door. The dance floor stayed packed, and the indoor pool stayed full of beautiful women from all over the Midwest. To my surprise, my cousin Earl was living up to his expectations and bringing some of the money back.

It was in July when I had to go to Oakland for training camp to pass the physical. I took Spaz with me just to have some company. I had ballooned up to 310 pounds but was still solid and in good-enough shape to pass. John Gruden had taken over as head coach of the Raiders, and they just acquired a young shutdown cornerback named Charles Woodson. I was excited with expectations of playing in Oakland. I even reunited with some of my old friends.

Spice one showed Spaz and I around before we left for home. When Spaz and I got off the plane in St. Louis, we were immediately stopped and asked to be searched at the baggage pickup area. I couldn't believe it! We were both clean and let go after being taken in a room a thoroughly searched.

I didn't think anything of it until I got back to the restaurant, and Ron told me that the inspectors came to make sure the restaurant passed all regulations and then wanted to check the book. I found that strange. I knew beating my case would make the Feds watch me like a hawk, but I was a marked man.

I was glade the football season was about start and I would be in Oakland.

Chapter 16

Out in the Bay

All work and no play makes Jack a dull boy, but all play and no work makes him some greatly worse.

—Samuel Jackson

My agent, Harold Lewis, was able to get me a two-year deal for 2.4 million and a couple of bonuses for signing and passing the physical. I decided to change my number to 93 because 99 wasn't a good number for me. Marc Trestman was the assistant coach. I knew him from Minnesota. Chuck Bresnahoen was one defensive coordinator, and the great Willie Brown from Grambling, who played with Denver and ended his Hall of Fame career with the Raiders as a defensive back, was one too. With Jon Gruden taking over as a coach, this meant that the defense would get better because he took pride in defense.

I didn't play that much during preseason. What I did was found an apartment not too far from the stadium since Shavonne was still staying at the house back in St. Louis. Our opening game was on the road against the Kansas City Chiefs. We got beat 28–8. I stopped by the house and spent some time with Shavonne before going back to Oakland.

The following weeks to come, I felt lonely without Shavonne, so when the team went on the road to play Dallas, I was ready to have some fun. I knew a few women from Dallas area that I could get up with and found them easily. I invited two of them to my suite and had a ménage à trios. The next game was in Arizona, and I had a ball out there too. When I got back to Oakland, I was tired. I decided to rest up and visit my dad the next day.

I went to South Central the following day. My cousin, Darryl, who was about my age, took me all around LA. I met a girl when we went to Venice Beach to see some comedians perform. She was very close to my height. Her name was Shelia. She had a caramel complexion and was attending Cal Berkley College. She played on the basketball team and was starting at forward. Her major was humanities. I would let her stay with me on Friday and Saturday in my Oakland apartment during my home games. Shelia was down for whatever. She would make me get up and jog with her on Saturday mornings and would watch all my games on television. Then she would give me constructive criticism about my game. She gave me space when I was talking on the phone to my other women too.

By the end of the season, I had another girlfriend named Jennifer who lived in Oakland. She was a redbone freak whose main hobby was having sex. The ironic thing about her was I met her when I went to church with a few of the players on the team. She worked in a day care center part-time.

California was turning out to be a place I wouldn't mind calling home. The only thing was that they stopped partying too early. Everything shut down at 1:00 a.m. My favorite spots were Oak Tree Paradise in Almino and Talk of the Town in San Jose.

When the season was over, I went back to St. Louis to be with Shavonne. We picked up where we had left off and had beautiful sex just about every night. Ron was running "The Legends" successfully, and I didn't have to worry about it. Most of my problems came when I went to visit in East St. Louis and ran into Corry. She was upset that I wasn't calling her when I was away, and when I was back in town, I wasn't spending time with her. I decided to stay away from her the whole spring.

Just before the summer came, I decided to make a major move. I came home from "The Legends" late Thursday night. Shavonne was in bed with the television on.

I came in the bedroom, and she looked at me and said, "Where you been? I've been calling you, and you haven't called me back."

"I know. I was thinking."

"Thinking! What were you thinking about that was too important to all me and let me know you were all right?"

I walked over to her and pulled out a little box from my pocket and said, "I was thinking about would you marry me?"

Shavonne's eyes got bright, and her mouth was gaped open as she heard me say the words. "James. Of course, I'll marry you."

"I was trying to figure out if we should have a big wedding or a small one."

"Let's have a small one," she said, reaching up to kiss me.

The following day, we told our family about our plans. Shavonne's parents didn't like it. Her father said that I was not a responsible man. He'd read about me on the Internet. Shavonne's mother agreed with her husband, telling her that I had two children from two different women. Shavonne got upset with them and told them that she was marrying me with or without their approval.

To my surprise, Grandma didn't want me to marry Shavonne either. She told me it would be one of the worst mistakes of my life. She told me that I would always regret it. Now I don't listen to nobody but my grandmother usually, but she was wrong about this one. Shavonne and I decided to move and get married in California.

We went to look at a house in Santa Barbara. It had a state-of-the-art security and communications system. The real estate agent took us through the two-story mansion that included high glass ceilings, Maplewood floors, a stainless steel kitchen, four bedrooms, three and a half bathrooms, a swimming pool, and living, dining, breakfast, family, and office rooms too. We both liked what we saw and were ready to move in as soon as possible. When Shavonne and I got off the plane in St. Louis, she told me she was feeling tired and nauseous. I told her it was probably jet lag.

As we approached the gate and headed for the exit, two men walked up beside both of us and said, "Excuse me, sir. May I have a word with you?"

"For what?" I said.

"I just want to search your bags," one of them said, pulling out a badge.

"For what? That's illegal. He hasn't done anything. You're harassing him," Shavonne said.

"I assure you we're not. We have the right to search—"

"Where is your warrant?" Shavonne said. "I'm an attorney and I know my rights."

"It's all right," I said cooperating with them and walking to a small room that was located through a side door.

While one went through our bags, the other asked where we were coming from, but Shavonne answered him quickly by saying, "None of your business."

We left the room as soon as they finished.

Shavonne was upset and said, "I hope you take heed to that incident."

"What are you talking about? That's not the first time I've been stopped in this airport."

"Well, you should have told Hess. He would've filed a complaint, and they would have stopped harassing you."

"I ain't worryin' 'bout it."

"That's not the point," Shavonne said while stopping a cab for us by waving her hand in the air. She looked just like a professional lawyer with her two-piece dark-blue pinstripe skirt set on and lambskin briefcase.

I told the driver our destination, and we were heading for home as she explained to me about my rights.

We were marred in California on July 7, 1999, at the City Hall. She had everything planned. She had job set up at another firm in LA and knew a few people in Cali already. She had a few girlfriends she went to school with back in Chicago who were currently living there for a few years too. The firm in St. Louis wasn't ever going to make her a partner, so Shavonne wasn't hesitant in leaving.

We settled into our new house and was enjoying the married life. Shavonne was the one woman I knew I could spend the rest of my life with because she was grounded and appreciated the small things I did for her. She had a lot of confidence in herself and wasn't the jealous type. It was only our second week in our new house when we were watching the late-night news.

She said, "James, you'll never guess what happened today."

"You're right, I'm no psychic."

She sucked her teeth and said, "I went to the doctor and I'm six weeks pregnant."

"And you didn't know?"

"I've only been off birth control for ten months. I would miss my cycle a lot of times when I was on the pill. I haven't been sick, and I haven't gained any weight. The only thing I did notice was that it hurt a little when we made love. I thought you were just getting bigger or something, but the doctor reassured me that I'm pregnant and that more blood was in my cervix causing it to be swollen."

"You told him that I was hurting you?"

"Her. And yes. I wanted to know what was wrong with my body."

I looked at her and said, "Well, we have enough room in this house for a few babies to live with us. We don't even use all the rooms."

"I love you," she said, kissing me on my shoulder.

"I love you too," I said, kissing her on the lips.

We decided to go to Hawaii before the NFL season started because Shavonne had a vacation week left to take. I drove the Range Rover out to my apartment; Jennifer was inside with her best friend, Pam.

"I was expecting you here. I didn't see your car outside," I said.

"Yeah. I know. Pam had to drive me over here because my car is in the shop. I got in an accident."

"Did you get hurt?"

"No, I'm fine."

"Well, you two need to catch up on things. I'll talk to you later, Jen," Pam said.

"Nice seeing you, James."

"Yeah, you too," I said, watching Pam walk toward the door. She had a Valentine-shaped derriere.

When I looked back at Jennifer, she was staring at the floor with worry in her blue eyes.

"What's going on, Jen?"

"I missed you. You never even called me since you left."

"My bad, baby. You look good. You gained some weight?"

"A little. You can tell?"

"Not really. Your face is a little fatter."

"I'm pregnant," Jennifer said.

I didn't even respond. I looked at her breasts, and they even looked a little bigger.

"Well? What do you have to say?"

"How many months are you?"

"Almost three months," she said, standing up. She was still wearing heels and a Chanel outfit. She carried her pregnancy well. "I want you to know that I've been with you."

I started thinking about what Shavonne would do when she found out because I knew Jennifer wouldn't abort the baby. *How would Shavonne handle this?*

"Do you hear me, James?"

"Yeah, girl. We gotta talk. Sit down," I said.

Jennifer and I talked the whole night. I told her about everything and Shavonne, including our marriage and her pregnancy. I even told her we were going to Hawaii next week. She seemed to take it well. We even made love. She initiated it by rubbing her hands on my thighs while we were talking and then giving me some face. I took her in the bedroom and woke up late the next morning for minicamp. I was rushing out the apartment and promised her I'd never come back.

Chapter 17

Games People Play

It's not over until it's over.

—Yogi Berra

When I got home, Shavonne had the Stevie Wonder CD playing "St. Louis Blues." I walked in the family room and saw her lying down on the Swedish recliner with tears coming down her face.

"What's wrong with you?" I asked.

She looked at me real evil before finally saying, "Jennifer called here."

Damn! I said to myself. I wanted to tell her. I was going to wait after the Hawaii trip. "Yeah, what did she want?"

"I know, James. You don't have to act anymore."

"I just found out. It was a mistake."

"You having an apartment was a mistake too? Why are you doing this to me?"

"Listen to me, Vonne," I said sitting down beside her.

"Get away from me!" she yelled, sitting up.

"You trippin'."

"You're the one losing it. Just leave me alone now."

"Aiight. That's the way you want it," I said, standing up and walking out the house.

I drove back to the apartment in Oakland. It was almost 10:30 p.m. when I got there. I opened the door, and Jennifer was sprawled on the couch in a skimpy Victoria's Secret chemise, watching cable and eating peaches. I slammed the door and saw her jump.

"What the fuck is your problem!"

"What did I do?"

"Don't play dumb," I said standing over her. "You called Shavonne right after I left. You went and pressed redial on the phone and told her everything."

"You wasn't planning on telling her shit, James. I know you by now!"

"So you make my decisions for me now? Ger the fuck out my house!"

"I ain't going nowhere."

"You wanna make a bet," I said, picking her up.

She started crying. "James. I love you. Please don't do this to me. I'm scared," she said with tears streaming down her face.

I was lost for words and took her to the bedroom. I laid her down and said, "Why did you do it?"

"I was scared I was gonna lose you. I love you, James. I'm sorry."

I looked at her crying and felt sorry for her. I kissed her on the lips and said, "Don't cry."

She kissed me back and stuck her tongue in my mouth. Her body felt good against mine. Before I knew it, I was taking off my clothes, and we were making love.

I woke up early the next morning and called Shavonne. She had the answering machine on, so I got back in bed while Jennifer went to work. At 10:00 a.m., I tried again. The answering machine came on again. At noon, I called a couple of my boys and asked them what they were going to do. They were going to check out some drag racing. So I went with them and didn't get back to the apartment until 11:00 p.m. I came in drunk.

Jennifer looked at me said, "You were out drinking all day and wanna get in the bed with me? Go shower first. That alcohol smell is making me nauseous."

"I'll sleep in the living room," I said, going back in the other room and crashing on the sofa.

I woke up the next morning and took a shower. I knew I had to face the music. I couldn't keep playing games with Shavonne. I drove home, and when I went inside, she was in the kitchen cooking veal spaghetti.

"You decided to come home."

"Listen, Shavonne…"

"No, you listen, James," she said, putting the spoon down and standing akimbo. "I married you and came to live with you out here for better or worse. Not as a trophy to stay home while you run around town with these girls and play games. I love you, but I'm not going to put up with this lifestyle of yours."

"I should have told you about Jennifer. But I didn't know she would pull a stunt like she did. Listen, let's just go to Hawaii and we can talk when you get back."

"We can do that," she said, turning back around to finish cooking. "But last time I checked, it took two people to make a baby."

*****

We got off the plane at Honolulu's international airport and stayed in the Hawaiian Prince Hotel. Later that day, we went to the Ukulele Festival. When we got back from the festival, we stayed in our hotel room and made love the rest of the day. The second day, we went snorkeling around early noon. When we came back to our room, Shavonne was complaining that she wasn't feeling good from the snorkeling and needed to lie down for a while. I went out and did some sightseeing and let her rest until the evening. When I woke her up, I showed her the Bermuda short sets I bought for us to wear to the luau.

There were over fifty people seated at the table with us. The bongos were being played to the rhythm of our heartbeats until a Polynesian man dressed in nothing but a grass skirt came out and started eating fire and spitting flames out of his mouth. I looked over a Shavonne, and she was enjoying the show as the fire-eating man was replaced by a bunch of girls dancing to the rhythm of the bongos with Hula-Hoops. I was on my second drink by the time they were grabbing people from the table to Hula-Hoop. Shavonne begged me to try it, so I did. I couldn't hold it upon my waist for nothing but wouldn't give up, so one of the girls came to show me how to do it.

When we started eating, Shavonne was sampling just about every Polynesian dish. I didn't know she could eat like that. When we got back to our room, we were both tired. We laid down with her head on my chest talking, and I don't remember when we fell asleep.

I was awakened by her voice, "James...James."

"Yeah," I said, letting out a stretch.

"Something's wrong."

"What do you mean?"

"I don't feel good. Every time I try to get up, I feel dizzy."

I got up and helped her to her feet. I walked her to the bathroom and let her put cold water on her face.

That's when she jerked in pain and grabbed her stomach. "James! Oh, God, please help me," she said, holding onto the sink.

I picked her up and took her back to the bed and dialed the reception desk. I asked for the nearest medical facility and was told it was only a half mile away. I got her there in fifteen minutes. The nurses tended to her immediately.

A Polynesian doctor came out after close to an hour and said, "Are you related to Mr. Harris?"

"Yeah, I'm her husband."

"Well, she going to be fine, but she just lost twin fetuses. I think the cause appears to be stress related."

"Can I go see her?"

"You may go see her, but she's on medication and sleeping at the moment," the doctor said as I walked toward the room she was in.

I looked at Shavonne lying on the hospital bed; she had lost color in her face. I could see she had been vomiting too. I couldn't believe what the doctor just told me. I knew it was my fault that she lost the babies. She was stressing because of me.

*****

Just before the season started, I went back to East St. Louis to make sure the restaurant was fine. Shavonne stayed at home and didn't go to work. She was still recovering. She was upset with me but wasn't admitting it as of yet. I was kind of glad to get away from her mood swings.

I visited Michelle and my son Kyle as soon as I got home. He was getting big. He was eleven years old and could hold a conversation with me. I wish I could introduce him to his brother, but I didn't even know how he looked. As long as Bonnie was getting the alimony, she didn't bother to stay in contact with me. After visiting family and taking care of my restaurant, I decided to go see Corry. As always, when I pulled up in front of the house, somebody was looking out the window. I got out the car and could tell it was Torry.

"Where's your sister?" I asked.

"She's at work."

"Where you goin'?"

"I was going out. It's boring here," Torry said, picking up some lint off her silk blouse.

I was wearing slip-on gators and a pair of jeans and said, "You wanna go to the Lou with me?"

"Yeah. Let's go," she said, walking to the passenger side of the Lincoln Continental rental I was driving.

When we got to St. Louis, I went straight to a bar called "Illusions." Everybody was glad to see me. I bought a case of Moet for everybody to drink in the bar. Torry and I sat off in a booth on the side to talk. She told me that her sister was upset about me leaving the state and getting married. I told her about Jennifer getting pregnant and calling Shavonne to lose the twins. I bought another case of Moet just as a friend I hadn't seen in a long time walked in.

"A. B., what's goin' on?" I said.

"Same ole shit. What you doin' in here?"

"A few drinks."

"That a whole lot of fews," A. B. said, looking at the case being put on top of the counter.

"Yeah, he been in here showing his Black ass," a dude said, who was sitting at the bar drinking.

"Yeah. Clause, I can do that. I'm the king of St. Louis."

"I wouldn't give a fuck if you were the queen of St. Louis," the short stocky man said.

I went toward him, and A. B. grabbed me and said, "Cool out, James."

Everybody in the bar had their attention on us.

I looked at the man and said, "You ain't worth it."

"Fuck you! You punk-ass nigga."

Before I could get to him, Torry came over and hit him in the head with a bottle of Moet. A. B. turned around and that's when I rushed the dude and body-slammed him to the floor.

Torry was kicking him in the face when another dude came over and grabbed her and said, "Get off him. That's enough."

I hit him so hard in the face I heard him scream as he fell to the floor. Torry and I left from the bar and went back to East St. Louis.

The following day, I was going back to Cali. Corry called me at 9:00 a.m. I had to catch a plane at eleven.

"I missed you yesterday."

"Yeah. Me and your sister hung out."

"I heard. Everybody thinks it was me and you that tore up the bar."

"Yeah," I said smiling. "Listen, I gotta go catch a flight."

"I know. You ain't got time for me."

"It's not like that, Corry. You could've been with me, but you didn't want to leave here. I can't live here."

"I understand. Call me whenever you come back," she said, hanging up on me before I could respond.

I got on the plane thinking about Corry. I loved her but she was too insecure, and I was getting tired of dealing with the insecurity. I took my set on the plane, and since no one sat next to me, I fell asleep when we were in the air. I changed planes in Minnesota and ended up on a full flight, so I sat next to a White man who was reading a *Fortune* magazine.

"Excuse me," I said as I passed him to sit by the window in first class.

"James Harris, right?"

"Yeah. That's me," I said, looking at the man I didn't know and couldn't remember.

"How you doing?"

"I'm doing all right."

"I'm sorry, you never met me. My name's Peter. I'm very good friend of Harold."

He knew my agent. What coincidence that I sat right next to him on a flight to LA.

I shook his hand and said, "Harold, huh? You must be an agent."

"No. That's not my profession at all. I'm a stockbroker."

I looked at the man real close as he spoke. He looked to be in his forties and was wearing an expensive suit and had a Johnston Murphy on his feet. No wedding or sign of hiding one on his finger.

"That's interesting because Harold is always trying to tell me to invest some money in something new, but I like to play it safe."

"I know, I know. Nobody likes to take risks when investing their money. I'm very good at finding junk bonds," Peter said, looking me straight in the eyes.

"They are the riskiest," I said as he started going through his briefcase that was in the seat between us.

As we were in the air, Peter showed me some junk bonds he invested in and their quarterly profits. Then he showed me a steel company that he was investing in that got my attention.

"Could I get a portfolio on this steel company?"

"Sure. I'll have to fax you one. How can I reach you?"

"Here. These are my cell and home numbers," I said, reaching in my pocket for my wallet and handing him a card with my information.

When I got home, Shavonne was talking on the phone as I came into the bedroom.

I put my luggage down, and she said, "I'll see you soon. Love you too," and hung up the phone.

"Who was that?" I asked.

"My mother. My parents are coming to visit me in a couple of weeks."

"I won't be here."

"And why not?" Shavonne said, standing akimbo.

"The season is about to start. I got two road games," I said, heading to the bathroom.

When I came out, she was doing her toes on the bed. I could tell she was ready to start arguing.

"I bet you got enough time to go to Oakland and see that White bitch."

"You don't even know what you're talkin' 'bout."

"I don't, huh? I know you wasn't in St. Louis all that time. She hasn't called hear one time since you been gone. That can only mean one thing."

Now I knew that Shavonne didn't trust me. I didn't have the patience for her tantrum, so I ignored her and left the room. That only made matters worse because she followed me.

"You'd rather be with that bitch than your wife," Shavonne said, trailing behind me as I went downstairs.

She would throw the Jennifer dilemma in my face every time she got a chance just to make me feel guilty and sorry for her. I wasn't ready to give up on us yet, but I didn't want this thrown in my face every time something didn't go her way either.

The first few weeks of the season, I stayed away from home on purpose. I spent time on the road with the team and with Jennifer in the Oakland apartment. I was giving Shavonne some space. I would talk to her on the phone and listen to her whine about being at home by herself, so I went home to be with her on her birthday in October. We went out to eat, and to my surprise, we had a good conversation. Her attitude was a whole lot better. When we got home, we made passionate love together.

The following weeks, we acted like we were a happily married couple. Peter had sent the portfolio to my house, and she wanted to help me look over the steel company. I had made up my mind to take Shavonne to meet the other NFL wives of the Raiders at a dinner regime fundraiser that was being held for breast cancer at a country club in San Ramon. She enjoyed herself and exchanged numbers with a few of the wives while I played golf.

After Thanksgiving, the team realized that we were teetering with the playoffs. We were heading to Mile High Stadium to play the Denver Broncos on Monday Night Football. The thing about mile high stadiums is the thin air. By the third quarter, you may need an oxygen tank. But on Monday night, the temperature was below freezing. We stepped on the field to a hostile crowd yelling at us from their seats. The Broncos had won the Super Bowl last year but was not even going to make the playoffs this year. They were trying to beat us simply because we were rivals.

The game was full of turnovers from the beginning. Finally, we scored first when Gannon connected with Tim Brown, but the Broncos came right back and scored. Then they managed to kick two field goals. We got one field goal, making the score 13-10 in favor of Denver at the half. The second half, we struck quickly with our hurry-up defense and scored a touchdown. We recovered a fumble but couldn't capitalize. We missed a field goal. The Broncos came back and scored 19-17 in their favor. As the clock ticked, we had the ball in their territory with the clock under two minutes. We worked the ball down to their thirty-three yard line and were ready to attempt a field goal with the clock down to three seconds. The kick went up and wide left as the clock expired. Our season was just about over now.

As I was leaving the field, somebody was yelling from the stands, "Aye, Harris! Get the fuck on the field and go sell drugs!"

I stopped for a moment and didn't bother to respond. I held my middle finger up toward the direction it came from.

*****

I decided to invest in the steel company and some junk bonds that Peter had suggested in December. My agent was going to have to get me another two-year deal with the Raiders because my contract was over after the season ended.

It was after the holiday season when I came home on Thursday evening after getting a haircut, and Shavonne was home from work already. She was sitting in the kitchen, reading an *Essence Magazine* when I walked in.

"You're home early," I said.

"Yeah. I need to talk to you about something very important."

"What is it?" I asked going to the refrigerator and pulling out a bottle of apple juice.

"I want a divorce."

I kept drinking juice as if I didn't hear her. When I stopped, I said, "Are you serious?"

"Yes, James. I got the papers and everything written up for the grounds I'm filing on. You want them now?"

"Where are they?" I said, looking at this shrewd bitch.

She strutted off sexy in her heels and pinstripe skirt set to retrieve her briefcase in the living room. When she came back, she gave me the papers and told me everything she expected was there. I couldn't believe it. She wanted half.

I got a California lawyer the following week and let him look at the papers. He told me that it was professionally done and that I should cooperate because under the California law, I didn't have a chance. Shavonne had hired a private investigator to follow me around while I was traveling to different cities playing football. She had pictures of me and Jennifer and had proof that Jennifer got pregnant by me after our marriage. She even had pictures of me and some of my teammates taking strippers and groupies back to our hotel. I said "fuck it" and decided whatever happens will happen and called my partner Spaz in East St Louis. I took him to Atlanta to see the Super Bowl.

We got in Atlanta on Friday and went to Jazzy T's; it was jam-packed. My favorite strippers were there. A girl name Stadia, who had a butterscotch complexion and a smile that could light up a room without a light bulb, and Devine, who was light skinned with a jelly booty and a small waist. Spaz was chasing behind a little petite girl name Li'l Cat. He spent over five hundred dollars on her just lap dancing with him and couldn't get her number.

We left there and went to Club 112. Luke was throwing a pre-Super Bowl party there. As soon as we got inside, Luke was on stage offering any female to give some brother some head, and they would be able to go to his Super Bowl after-party and to Cancun for free. There were females waving their hands to be chosen, but one sister with full lips and a perfect weave was chosen. She went on stage and whipped the brother's dick out and started giving it mouth to mouth.

Spaz looked at me and back at the stage. Then he said, "Let's get closer."

We went as close as we could, and the sister stopped and said, "He can't even get hard. Look at it."

You could hear roars of laughter inside the club and then a bunch of brothers yelling, "Let me take his place!"

We went to the Georgia Dome on Sunday to see the St. Louis Rams play the Tennessee Titans in Super Bowl XXIV. The Rams won 23-16 in a game that came down to the last play.

I brought Spaz back to LA with me and showed him around. We went to all the strip clubs. First Kings and then Peanuts, which ended up being his favorite spots. Spaz stayed with me for a month before going back home.

In March, I went with Peter to check out some sites where the steel company had investments we went to Tijuana, Mexico. From there, we went back to LA and had to go to Utah the following week. After the Utah meeting, I was convinced to get involved in the street business.

It was April when Harold Lewis got in contact with me about my new contract with the Raiders. He promised me that he would get the same contract as before. I went to see him at his office early Monday, and he was in a happy mood.

"Harris. It's good to see you. Have a seat," he said as he sipped on a mug. "You want some coffee?"

"No thanks," I said as I sat down.

He pulled some papers out and said, "I couldn't get the contract redone, but I managed to get you one more bonus for not missing a game that will put you at over two million."

I was reading the papers as he was talking to me. I could see that I was half a million short. I could make a quarter of a million if

I didn't miss a game every year, which would make back up half million, but I wasn't receiving any bonuses for my physical or anything else for that matter, which made my money short. On top of it, after one minor injury, I would be out of a quarter of a million dollars. I complained but signed the contract anyway. I had a divorce case coming up in June and needed the income.

In the middle of April, Jennifer had the baby. I was not there to see her have the baby girl. She named her Kiara Harris. She was happy that I was getting a divorce because she thought she had a chance to be with me.

In June, I went to divorce court. I put a "for sale" sign up on the house in Santa Barbara and moved to Ontario, California. I looked at Shavonne who had a way of smiling without showing it on her face. At one time, I liked that quality in her but not as the evidence was being presented to the judge by her lawyer. The court awarded her half. She became a millionaire just by divorcing me.

When I got home, to my surprise, Peter called me and said, "I need to see you. I have a check for you. I pulled out one of my stock investments."

"How about tomorrow morning I'll stop by your office?"

"That'll be fine. See you tomorrow," he said, clicking off from me.

I went by his office the next day, and Peter handed me a check for two hundred thousand. I didn't ask any questions. I left the office a half hour later and decided to go see the Sugar Shane Mosley and De La Hoya fight in Vegas. I called Spaz and told him to take a flight to LA. We were going to Vegas.

By the time July came around, I was thinking about minicamp. I wasn't ready at all. I'd seen Peter a week before, and he gave me a check for 110,000 dollars for another twelve thousand-dollar investment on a junk bond. He was definitely the man. I was still drinking and working out as of yet.

By the time preseason started, I was getting molded into shape with The Stone, Lance Johnston. We determined to have a good season, and that's just what we did. We went 13-4. Rich Gannon had an MVP season and shared the honors with Marshall. We went to the playoffs and shut out Miami 27-0 but lost AFC championship to Baltimore 16-3. Ray and the Ravens had raised the bar on playing defense that season. They went on to win Super Bowl XXXV 34-7 against the NY Giants in Tampa.

The next season I was looking forward to because we knew we were only one step away from the Super Bowl. We had a great defense. The previous season, Charles made the pro bowl team. Eric had played good with all the pressure on him because quarterbacks didn't want to try Charles on the other side, and Grady had the most sacks with the defensive front line we had. We had Jerry along with Tim, Jerry, and James at receiver. Tyron was our main ball carrier. This was the first season I was totally committed to playing football. I still had my harem of girlfriends, but they didn't affect my concentration of the game. We got our revenge on the first few weeks against the Ravens on Sunday night. Gannon picked their defense apart. Our defense shut their offense down.

We made a statement and put on an offensive display the first four games. The Oakland Raiders were making it to the Super Bowl and would not be stopped.

In October, the players threw a Halloween party in Oakland at a club called Oaktree. I invited Spaz down. I dressed up in a number 75 jersey and bought a gold cap for my tooth and put a pillow in my stomach. I was going as Brady Jackson. When Spaz and I got there, it was crowded, and it was only 8:30 p.m. I had sent Jennifer to the airport to pick up two of my friends. One of the women was my girlfriend named Mona. The other girl was Yvette. When Jennifer brought them to the party, Spaz and I were dancing with some girls I knew from Detroit. They were cool with me. Spaz was liking the one named Terry but could tell she wasn't feeling him. Jennifer caught my eye as I was dancing, and I excused myself and went over to them, leaving Spaz behind with Terry.

"Hey, James. Why couldn't you come pick us up?" Mona said.

I sized both of them up. They were dressed in similar skirts. Mona had on more jewelry, and her body was busting out of her skirt. Yvette was a very pretty girl. They both did a lot of small-time modeling. They were almost six feet tall too.

"I was busy," I said with an attitude.

"What's wrong with you?" Mona asked.

I looked at Jennifer, and she was trying to act like she wasn't paying us no attention.

"Nothin'. I'm going to party," I said, walking away and going back to the Detroit girls and dancing.

After a good amount of time went by, Mona and Yvette came over and introduced themselves to the Detroit girls. I moved around but could tell they were cool with each other before I left.

When it got close to 1:00 a.m., Jennifer told me she was going back to the apartment and that I should use the other apartment to take my guests. Spaz, Mona, Yvette, and I went to my other apartment until the morning. Nothing happened sexually between us because Spaz wasn't feeling Yvette and vice versa. Besides, Mona had an attitude, and I wasn't in the mood to deal with it.

I woke up the following morning and called Jennifer. I talked to her loud enough for Mona to overhear and said, "Stop by the ATM and get some money so that you can drive these girls to the airport and buy them tickets."

Later on that day, Terry called me to ask about Spaz. Before I gave him the phone, she asked me about Mona and Yvette. I told her that Jennifer took them to the airport and bought them plane tickets back to LA. Terry started laughing and then heard her telling her Detroit girlfriends the story. All I could hear in the background was that I did some gangsta shit.

Peter never stopped coming through for me with checks. Even as the season was coming close to an end, we had on through the injury bug but still managed to be in the first place in our division. The Super Bowl was ours. We could taste it. We were in the playoffs and would just have to win two games to make it to big party.

We were right back where we started in the AFC championship after routing Pittsburgh. This time, our opponent was the New England Patriots. We were in the Foxboro Stadium playing in the snow. It was just below thirty-two degrees. Everybody knew we preferred not to play in the snow, but in the order to get to the Super Bowl, we didn't have a choice.

The veterans held the team together all season and made big plays. Now it was time for everybody to contribute. It was only 6-3 New England at the half. When we came out on the field for the second half, it started snowing harder. This made or vision blurry, and it was hard to move laterally. Tom took advantage of this and used a lot of play action, but we had a reliable secondary with Eric, Charles, and Rod. We managed to tie the game when Jankowski kicked a twenty-seven-yard field goal to the end the third quarter. With the score tied 6-6 in the fourth quarter, we struck the end zone first with Tyrone. We were now p 13-6 with the extra point kicked in.

It was under six minutes to play, and we had the ball trying to eat the clock up. We were on the Patriots forty-five yard line when we had to kick the ball back to them. They got the ball on the twenty after the touchback. The clock was down to three and a half minutes. Once again, Tom mixed it up with play action and no huddle offense. We were in our present defense, so they were moving the ball slowly but safely down the field. The two-minute warning came, and they were close to the fifty-yard line. Our defense came to the side, and we got together and talked like never before. We could taste the Super Bowl, and we wanted it.

"The middle linebacker must stay home from here on out," Russell Maryland said.

Our cornerbacks were good enough to stay on man-to-man coverage with the safeties having to know if to blitz or stop the run. We were all focused and ready when we went back on the field. The Patriots got to our thirty-one-yard line with a little over a minute to go. That's when we knew it was all or nothing.

The next two plays, we shut the Patriots down leaving them at third and a long eight yard. Tom dropped back to pass, and I saw him about to throw the ball. I was so close but yet too far away to stop him. The next thing I knew, I saw the ball dropping out of his hand. I immediately dived on it, and there was a pile up on me.

I could hear Big Russell yelling, "It's me on top of you, James!"

I got up with the ball and gave it to the referee, and our defense ran to the sidelines. We did it! We were heading to the Super Bowl. New England didn't have any more time-outs to stop us from running out the clock. Before the offense took the field, New England threw their flag out to review the play. This delayed the game for a while. The referees were finally ready to state their call. When they said that was an incomplete pass and not a fumble, I couldn't believe it.

"That's bullshit!" Jon spat.

I knew they weren't going to change the call and so did everybody else, including the fans who were cheering the call on. They claimed Tom's arm was forward when the ball came out of his hand.

The next play was forth down and eight yards to go for the Patriots. Tom got in shotgun and threw the ball. I could see Charles was being tried. When the ball hit the ground, we knew it was over, but the referee threw a flag and called defensive pass interference. The ball was placed on the one yard line. We tried to stop them but couldn't. They scored and tied the game up on a Tom sneak. We now had to win the coin toss and did. The only thing about it was we didn't move the ball down the field and had to punt it to the Patriots, who moved the ball down field and kicked a field goal to win 16–13 in overtime. The season had to end like that. I felt we were cheated out of the game.

During the off-season, I got more into the steel company. I would still hang out and go to the clubs, but I was serious about my investments. Peter was onto something in the stock market, so I just kept receiving money from him just about every four months.

One summer day when I was coming from visiting my father in east LA, I ran into Mona and one of her friends, Sunny, on Crenshaw Boulevard. I was driving the Lexus and honked the horn at them in their Toyota Passport.

"How you doing, James?" Sunny said from behind the wheel.

"Pull over," I said.

They pulled over, but I could tell Mona had an attitude as I approached their car.

"How have you been, Sunny?" I said, ignoring Mona.

"I'm fine. It's been a while since I saw you. Mona hasn't been saying anything about you."

I looked at Mona and said, "Whassup, girl."

"Hi, James," she said with no enthusiasm.

Sunny knew something wasn't right and said, "I'll talk to you later. We're kind of in a rush."

"Aiight," I said, heading back to my car.

I called Sunny that night and we talked for an hour. She was surprised I still had her number. She told me she didn't know that Mona and I had stopped seeing each other until today. I told her my version since she had already heard Mona's version.

She put it together and said, "Y'all wasn't right for each other anyway."

"You're right. Maybe we're right for each other," I said, dead serious.

Sunny picked up on what I said, and I could tell she was blushing on the phone. She was by far the finest out of all the girlfriends. She had dimples to go with her smile. I could tell when she first met me, she was wondering what I was doing with Mona. We decided to start seeing each other. And that's what we did the whole summer.

When minicamp started, I was ready to be devoted to the team this season. I finally had a woman who I was comfortable with. She was all I needed. Sunny was godsent.

The first day of minicamp, I came in weighing 325 pounds. I knew I had to lose some weight, but I had time. I was talking to Russell and Eric about my agent playing Jordan and I on our contracts but cutting a deal with G. M. Bruce to get us pay cuts, but he still kept his percentage. When I noticed G-Men coming for me, I was driving and calling my lawyer at the same time.

"Hey, Mr. Finnigan, I was at football practice and saw some Feds."

"Yeah, Mr. Harris. They just informed me an hour ago that they are going to arrest you."

"For what?"

"I'm not sure. Where are you?"

"On the way to your office. I think they're behind me," I said, hanging up the phone.

I got to Mr. Finnigan's office, and the Feds came about ten minutes later. I was being arrest for stock fraud.

Chapter 18

Here and Now

Never forget a saint is a sinner who keeps on trying.

—Nelson Mandela

I was sentenced to twenty-seven months and given a three million-dollar fine under Title 18, Section 1957: *The Willful Blindness Statue*. This was similar to money laundering. I was accepting money from my broker (Peter Sherman) but did not know where it was coming from. Over three million dollars made it a big case of insider trading. I was offered a deal by the government to help catch a few people. They tried scaring me by showing me pictures they had of me in Vegas and Atlanta with various hustlers, ballers, and shot callers. I pled the fifth but not before I asked for one of the pictures they had of me with a Black stripper who had the prettiest skin I've ever seen. Of course, they didn't give it to me.

I was glad it was over, to tell you the truth. I was tired of playing the cat-and-mouse game. Things happen for a reason. This time, what I got was a blessing in disguise. It helped me become a better man spiritually. I was caught up on the material and physical world so much that I forgot about knowledge of self. When you have money, you start to realize sooner or later that you can only do the same things over and over again to enjoy yourself. If you don't have money, you think it can solve problems, but once you have it and analyze your situation, it's not a means to an end, but it's an end of acknowledging self.

I could see the sunlight coming through the window. It reminds me that I have brighter days ahead. My girl Sunny is home waiting for me still. The two divorces helped me grow into a better man, and now I'm ready for a monogamous relationship.

Some people may say that I was ignorant, naïve, greedy, or a loser. But you have to be ignorant before you can learn something. You have to be naïve before you experience fem, and you have to be greedy when you are around a lot of things and you never had to appreciate where you came from. Most importantly, you have to be a loser in order to understand how to be a winner.

About the Author

James Harris is a father of five exceptional athletes with shocking abilities showcased as early as the age of seven years old. Due to his outstanding play on the field, James was able to receive an athletic scholarship, graduate Temple University, and play professionally in the NFL. James, also a former high school coach at East St. Louis High, has a passion for helping others in need during tough times. During his tenure in the NFL, James started a nonprofit organization (Families of America) in which he helped build single-family homes for minorities. Having always had faith but fully committing his life to God in his thirties, James is a true servant to the Lord, thankfully with the help of Southern Mission Baptist Church and Rev. Jerome Jackson of East St. Louis.

Printed in the USA
CPSIA information can be obtained
at www.ICGtesting.com
LVHW091039310324
775985LV00023B/201